CHILDREN'S
ENCYCLOPEDIA
OF SHARKS

Claudia Martin

ARCTURUS

ARCTURUS

This edition published in 2022 by Arcturus Publishing Limited
26/27 Bickels Yard, 151–153 Bermondsey Street,
London SE1 3HA

Author: Claudia Martin
Designer: Lorraine Inglis
Consultant: Jules Howard

ISBN: 978-1-3988-2017-3
CH010270NT
Supplier 29, Date 0722, PI 00000997

Printed in China

CHILDREN'S
ENCYCLOPEDIA
OF SHARKS

CONTENTS

Super Sharks

Sharks are an extraordinary group of fish. Some sharks are famed for their ferocity, while others are known for their great size or speed. Nearly all sharks are meat-eaters, swallowing animals from seals to seabirds and shrimp to other sharks.

The little gulper shark hunts for fish and squid in coastal waters.

Hunters

Most sharks are hunters, using their keen senses to track down prey. The majority of fish have small brains compared to their body size, but sharks have fairly large brains. Having a larger brain helps sharks to make sense of information from their senses. It also helps them plan where and how to catch prey. A few sharks can even work with other members of their group to corner and catch prey.

This small shark grows up to 1 m (3.3 ft) long.

Of all the sharks, the shortfin mako shark has one of the largest brains compared to its body size. It stalks its prey unnoticed, waiting for a moment when fish are weakest.

Habitats

Most sharks live in the oceans, but a few can survive in both salty ocean water and freshwater rivers. Sharks are found in all oceans, from warm tropical waters through cooler temperate seas to the cold polar zone. Sharks are common fish down to 2,000 m (6,560 ft) beneath the ocean surface. A few sharks are known to swim as deep as 3,000 m (9,840 ft). While some sharks are found in the open ocean, far from land, others live only in coastal habitats, including coral reefs and seagrass meadows.

Around 64 cm (25 in) long, the blind shark lives in seagrass meadows on the eastern coast of Australia.

Its green eyes are large, helping it to see in the dim water up to 1,400 m (4,600 ft) beneath the ocean surface.

Humans

Since humans first journeyed over the oceans, we have been fascinated by sharks. From the islands of the Pacific Ocean to the coasts of Africa, people's fear and wonder of sharks led them to worship shark gods. In more recent times, movies have told tales of terrifying sharks with a taste for human flesh. Yet the truth is that sharks have far more to fear from humans than we do from them. Today, sharks are at risk due to human activities from fishing to construction.

Divers take a close look at a great white shark while protected by a cage.

What Is a Shark?

Like all fish, sharks can breathe underwater, have scale-covered skin, and use their fins for swimming. Yet while most fish have skeletons made of bone, sharks and their relatives have skeletons made of cartilage.

A Shark Skeleton

Cartilage is a body material that is less hard than bone, but much more bendy and lightweight. Humans have cartilage in places such as their outer ears and the tip of their nose. Cartilage makes a shark's skeleton lighter than those of similarly sized fish, so it can use less energy to swim. In addition, cartilage helps a shark to twist and turn easily.

A shark has no ribcage to protect its organs, but its fins are supported by cartilage.

Great white shark

LARGEST SHARKS

Whale shark: Up to 18.8 m (61.7 ft) long
Basking shark: Up to 12.3 m (40.3 ft) long
Greenland shark: Up to 6.4 m (21 ft) long
Great white shark: Up to 6.1 m (20 ft) long
Great hammerhead shark: Up to 6.1 m (20 ft) long

DID YOU KNOW? Sharks have no ribcage, so if they wash up on shore their organs can be crushed by the weight of their body.

A whale shark can weigh around 19,000 kg (42,000 lb), which is more than 270 adult men.

Biggest and Smallest

The largest shark is also the world's largest fish. The whale shark can grow up to 18.8 m (61.7 ft) long. It is found throughout the world's tropical oceans. In contrast, the smallest shark is found only along the coasts of Venezuela and Colombia, in South America. The dwarf lanternshark grows no longer than 20 cm (8 in). It is believed to live for 20 to 30 years, while its immense relative may live for up to 130 years.

Like all sharks, a blacktip reef shark has flexible jaws that are not attached to its skull, so it can shoot them forward to snap up prey.

Like most other fish, a Pacific double-saddle butterflyfish has a bony skeleton.

A close relative of sharks, a stingray also has a skeleton made of cartilage.

Anatomy

Most sharks have eight fins, but some have fewer. Like other fish, sharks breathe using gills. While the gills of most fish are protected by a bony cover, sharks have visible gill slits on either side of their head. Most sharks have five pairs of gill slits, but some have six or seven.

The Atlantic sixgill is a rare shark, found only in the warm waters of the western Atlantic Ocean.

Fins

All sharks have a pair of pectoral fins, on either side of their body behind their head. These large fins help with steering. On a shark's underside, it has a pair of pelvic fins, which aid stability by stopping sideways rolls. Most sharks also have a single anal fin closer to their tail, which improves stability. Sharks have either one or two dorsal fins on their upper side, with the first dorsal fin larger than the second. Dorsal fins keep the shark upright. The tail fin, known as the caudal fin, is moved from side to side to push the shark forward. The upper portion, or lobe, of the caudal fin is usually larger than the lower lobe.

First dorsal fin

Gill slits

Second dorsal fin

Caudal fin

Anal fin

A Caribbean reef shark has eight fins and five pairs of gill slits.

Pelvic fins

Pectoral fins

Tiger shark tooth

BIGGEST TEETH

Great white shark: 6.4 cm (2.5 in) long, around 250 at a time
Tiger shark: 5.1 cm (2 in) long, around 350 at a time
Sand tiger shark: 2.5 cm (1 in) long, around 150 at a time
Bull shark: 2.5 cm (1 in) long, around 350 at a time
Shortfin mako shark: 2 cm (0.8 in), around 100 at a time

The lower jaw of a kitefin shark has five rows of large, triangular replacement teeth behind its front teeth. This shark's powerful bite lets it feed on fish and octopus as well as take bites out of much larger animals, such as whales.

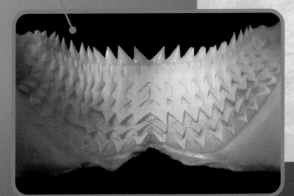

Tooth Factory

Whenever a shark's tooth falls out—due to biting bone or grasping wriggling prey—the tooth is replaced. A tooth is replaced every few days or weeks. Rows of replacement teeth grow in a groove inside the jaws. When a front tooth breaks, the teeth behind it move forward. The shape of a shark's teeth depends on its prey. Sharp teeth with jagged edges are ideal for slicing seal flesh, but wide, flat teeth are useful for crushing turtle shells.

It has a single, small dorsal fin, which is unusually close to its tail fin.

Unlike most sharks, this shark has six pairs of gill slits.

DID YOU KNOW? Ground sharks can grow as many as 35,000 teeth over the course of their life.

Skin

Shark skin is thicker than the skin of other fish, which helps protect sharks from attacks by predators. Their skin is also so rough that it can injure an attacker. Shark skin is almost entirely covered with special, toothlike scales known as dermal denticles.

Dermal Denticles

Sharks and their relatives have dermal denticles, which means "small skin teeth." These scales contain similar materials to human teeth, such as enamel, which makes them very hard. The scales are ribbed and pointed. When stroked backward, the scales are sharp, but they are flattened by the flow of water as a shark swims. The shape of the scales helps a shark to cut through the water swiftly and silently, so it can creep up on prey.

The banded wobbegong is nocturnal, doing most of its feeding at night.

Under a powerful microscope, we can see the dermal denticles of the small–spotted catshark. Each denticle is up to 1 mm (0.04 in) long.

Camouflage

Many sharks have patterned dermal denticles to help with camouflage. This lets them blend in with their surroundings, making them difficult for predators and prey to spot. In the carpet shark order, many sharks have bold patterns to blend in when lying among coral or on the seabed. Sharks that live in open water, such as the great white shark, may be countershaded, with pale undersides and darker backs. From below, the pale belly is hard to spot against the sunlight. From above, the shark blends into the darker depths.

The tasselled wobbegong is a carpet shark that is well camouflaged on coral reefs.

10

DEEPEST DIVES

Portuguese dogfish: 3,675 m (12,057 ft) deep
Cookiecutter shark: 3,505 m (11,500 ft) deep
Velvet belly lanternshark: 2,490 m (8,170 ft) deep
Greenland shark: 2,200 m (7,200 ft) deep
Pacific sleeper shark: 2,000 m (6,600 ft) deep

Greenland shark

This shark lies in wait as flaps of skin around its mouth drift in the water, attracting the attention of small prey.

Inside the mouth are more than 100 long, sharp teeth.

DID YOU KNOW? The skin of a whale shark is up to 15 cm (4 in) thick, the thickest of any animal.

11

Breathing

Like all animals, a shark needs a constant supply of oxygen for its organs to function. Water contains oxygen, which sharks take in using their gills. To breathe, sharks can open their mouth while swimming, so water flows inside, passes through the gills, and runs out of the gill slits.

Taking Oxygen

Like other fish, a shark uses its gills for taking in oxygen and getting rid of carbon dioxide, which is a waste product made by the body as it turns oxygen into energy. After water flows into a shark's mouth, it passes into the gills through openings at the sides of the mouth. The water flows over feather-like filaments that contain many tiny blood vessels. These have such thin walls that oxygen can pass through and into the shark's blood.

The coral catshark spends the daytime resting in crevices on coral reefs, in the Indian and Pacific Oceans.

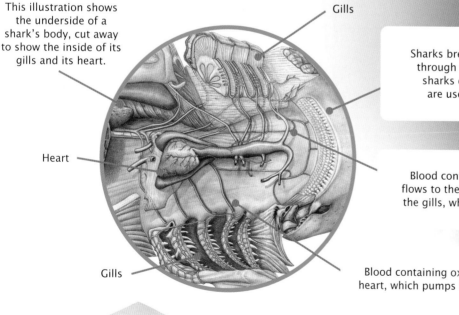

This illustration shows the underside of a shark's body, cut away to show the inside of its gills and its heart.

Gills

Heart

Gills

Sharks breathe by taking in water through their mouth. Although sharks do have nostrils, they are used only for smelling.

Blood containing carbon dioxide flows to the heart and is pumped to the gills, where the gas is released.

Blood containing oxygen flows to the heart, which pumps it around the body.

LONGEST LIVING SHARKS

Greenland shark: Over 270 years
Whale shark: Over 100 years
Bluntnose sixgill shark: Over 80 years
Great white shark: Over 70 years
Spiny dogfish: Over 45 years

Spiny dogfish

This seafloor-living shark uses its spiracle to suck in water when it is resting.

Water flows out of the gills through five pairs of gill slits.

Moving or Resting

When sharks are swimming swiftly, there is a constant flow of water into the mouth and through the gills. Most sharks can also suck water into their mouth when they are lying still. Slow-moving or seafloor-living sharks have holes known as spiracles, just behind their eyes, through which they can suck in extra water. However, a few sharks do not have the ability to suck in water, so they must swim constantly to stay alive. These sharks include the great white, hammerhead, and whale shark.

Although sharks do not sleep deeply like humans, they do have periods of rest when they are less alert, even though their eyes remain open. Sharks that can breathe while motionless may lie on the seafloor, like this Japanese bullhead shark.

DID YOU KNOW? Even when a great white shark is sleeping, it will continue to swim as its fin movements are automatic.

Swimming

Unlike most fish, a shark will sink if it stops swimming. This is useful for bottom-living sharks, but not so useful for sharks that hunt in open water. Yet sharks are expert swimmers, moving their fins to travel up, down, left, right, and forward—but never backward.

Staying Afloat

Fish with bony skeletons are able to float because of a gas-filled organ named a swim bladder, which acts like an air-filled rubber ring. Sharks do not have swim bladders. However, they do have a lightweight skeleton. In addition, they have a large liver, which is filled with oil. This oil is lighter than seawater, enabling a shark to float a little. Yet sharks would still sink slowly in the water, so they must swim constantly to stay at a particular depth, using the position of their pectoral fins to steer themselves upward.

A shark's pectoral fins function a little like the wings of a plane. The fins' shape and tilt make the water flow more quickly over them than beneath them. This puts greater water pressure on the underside of a shark's pectoral fins, pushing the shark upward.

FASTEST SWIMMERS

Shortfin mako shark: Up to 74 km/h (46 miles per hour)
Salmon shark: Up to 56 km/h (35 miles per hour)
Common thresher shark: Up to 48 km/h (30 miles per hour)
Great white shark: Up to 40 km/h (25 miles per hour)
Blue shark: Up to 39 km/h (24.5 miles per hour)

Thresher shark

DID YOU KNOW? The slowest shark, the Greenland shark beats its tail only 9 times per minute and reaches 3 km/h (1.9 miles per hour).

The tall dorsal fin acts as a pivot (like the middle point of a seesaw), letting the shark spin quickly around it.

A tiger shark swims by beating its tail from side to side.

Its long pectoral fins lift this shark—which weighs up to 635 kg (1,400 lb)—through the water.

No Going Back

Sharks have different styles of swimming, but no shark can swim backward. Solid-bodied sharks, such as great whites, swim by beating their large tail. Sharks with long, slender bodies, such as catsharks, also wiggle their body from side to side, like an eel. All these movements push a shark forward rather than backward. A shark's pectoral fins do not have the range of movement needed to paddle a shark backward. Sharks can move backward only by turning around or letting themselves drift.

A striped pyjama catshark wiggles its whole body in a wave-like motion.

Senses

Sharks have the same five senses as humans: sight, hearing, taste, smell, and touch. In addition, sharks can sense electrical currents and changes in water pressure. All these senses make sharks skilled hunters—as well as helping smaller sharks to escape attack.

The blue shark's sense of smell is less powerful than its eyesight, with only 3 percent of its brain dedicated to examining smells.

Seven Senses

1 **Sight:** A shark has eyes on the sides of its head, so it can see all around. At the back of each eye is a layer of shiny cells, which reflects light back into the eye, helping a shark to see in dark, deep water.

2 **Hearing:** A shark's ears are behind its eyes, visible from the outside as two small holes. Sharks are particularly good at hearing low sounds, such as the noises made by wounded prey.

3 **Taste:** Most sharks do not rely on taste to find prey, so this sense is usually less developed than the others. However, some sharks have barbels (see opposite). All sharks taste prey when they bite in, spitting out what they do not like.

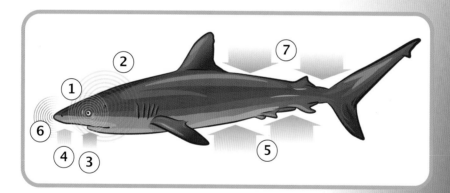

4 **Smell:** This sense is one of a shark's most powerful, with large parts of its brain devoted to identifying smells. Tiny particles given off by prey and predators float through the water to a shark's nostrils. A shark can sense the direction of a smell from the time that it reaches each nostril.

5 **Touch:** Nerves in a shark's skin and teeth carry signals about touch, temperature, and pain to its brain. The sensitivity of its teeth means that a shark often uses its mouth to find out more about objects.

6 **Electroreception:** A shark's snout and head have many tiny dips, or pores, known as ampullae of Lorenzini. These contain special cells that detect electric fields. As any animal's muscles move, they give off tiny electric charges. Sharks are more sensitive to these electric fields than any other animal.

7 **Pressure changes:** A line of pores, known as the lateral line, runs from a shark's snout to its tail. As water flows into these pores, special cells sense changes in the pressure of the water. This lets a shark detect moving prey and understand its surroundings, as its movement creates waves that bounce back off rocks and the seabed.

DID YOU KNOW? Around 18 percent of a great white shark's brain is dedicated to smell, giving it one of the most powerful senses of smell of all sharks.

With its two barbels, the zebra shark can hunt for small fish and shrimp at night.

Barbels

Some sharks have fleshy, finger-like body parts on their snout, known as barbels. These are sense organs a little like a cat's whiskers. Barbels are usually found on fish that live in murky water or hunt at night, helping them make up for loss of vision. Barbels have cells that detect particles that float from prey and predators, improving the closely linked senses of taste and smell.

Its eyes are large, so they can let in enough light for the shark to see in dim water as deep as 350 m (1,150 ft).

Ampullae of Lorenzini are dotted across the snout, helping the blue shark detect the movements of squid and octopus.

The bigeye thresher has the largest eyes of any shark, up to 10 cm (4 in) across.

SENSING PREY

Maximum distances for sharks

Smell: Up to 500 m (1,640 ft)
Hearing: Up to 240 m (790 ft)
Pressure changes: Up to 100 m (330 ft)
Sight: Up to 25 m (80 ft)
Electroreception: Up to 0.9 m (3 ft)

Feeding

Most sharks feed every two or three days. Although sharks are excellent at finding prey, their bodies are slow at digesting (breaking down) food, so they must wait between meals. All except three sharks are hunters that use their strong teeth for catching and killing.

Hunting Methods

Some sharks, such as great whites, use speed and strength to catch large prey. In contrast, seafloor-living sharks such as wobbegongs and angelsharks use camouflage and patience, lying in wait for prey, then making a sudden lunge. Sawsharks use their long snout to stir up small prey from the seabed, while thresher sharks stun fish with flicks of their large tail. Cookiecutter sharks rarely take whole prey, but feed on flesh bitten from living animals.

Copper sharks hunt in a group, working together to herd fish into a ball. Each shark takes turns to swim through the ball with its mouth open.

When a great white shark bites a fish, the strength of its jaws and sharpness of its teeth can kill instantly.

A copper shark grows up to 3.3 m (11 ft) long.

DID YOU KNOW? Copper sharks swim around fishermen in the hope of stealing their catches, even attempting to snatch fish from their hands.

Sharks most likely to bite humans: Great white shark, tiger shark, bull shark, oceanic blacktip shark, sand tiger shark

Provoked bites (when the person tried to touch or feed the shark): Usually under 50 per year

Unprovoked bites: Usually under 100 per year

Bull sharks occasionally bite humans out of curiosity, then spit them out.

Sardines make a yearly migration along the coast of South Africa, followed closely by copper sharks.

The basking shark has around 1,500 teeth, each around 0.5 cm (0.2 in) long, but they are not used for feeding.

Filter Feeding

Three of the largest sharks—whale, basking, and megamouth sharks—use a different method of feeding. Although these sharks have hundreds of teeth, they are tiny and not suited to catching and killing prey. Instead, these sharks fill their immense mouth with ocean water containing tiny creatures. The creatures are filtered out and swallowed, while the water flows out through the shark's gills.

19

Life Cycle

Some female sharks give birth to live babies, known as pups, while others lay eggs. All shark mothers have one thing in common: They do not take care of their pups. Yet newborn pups can already swim and hunt, giving them the skills needed to survive.

Laying Eggs

Around a third of sharks lay eggs, which is known as oviparity (meaning "egg birth"). Egg-layers include bullhead sharks and some catsharks. Shark eggs have a tough case to protect the unborn baby, known as an embryo, as it develops. Egg cases are often called mermaid's purses. Eggs are often laid in rocky crevices or among coral or seagrass, to which the egg cases attach with long, threadlike tendrils.

A swell shark embryo is growing inside its egg case, which is around 10 cm (4 in) long.

Over time, the egg inside an egg case develops into an embryo.

A yolk sac contains food for the swell shark embryo.

Great hammerhead pup

MOST LIVE PUPS

Whale shark: Litters of up to 300 live pups
Blue shark: Litters of up to 135 live pups
Tiger shark: Litters of up to 80 live pups
Great hammerhead: Litters of up to 55 live pups
Scalloped hammerhead: Litters of up to 40 live pups

The egg case will be home to the embryo for 9 to 12 months, after which it will break through the case using the extra-long dermal denticles on its back.

Lemon sharks are viviparous. Like a newborn human, a newborn lemon shark is still attached to its mother by a cord, through which it received food. The cord breaks as the pup swims away.

Live Pups

Female sharks give birth to live pups in one of two ways: viviparity or ovoviviparity. In viviparity (meaning "living birth"), babies develop inside their mother's body in a similar way to human babies. Viviparous sharks include hammerhead and requiem sharks. The majority of sharks are ovoviviparous. In ovoviviparity (meaning "egg living birth"), babies develop inside eggs, which hatch while they are still in the mother's body. The embryos continue to grow inside their mother until they are ready to be born, which can take up to 2 years. Mothers usually give birth to their pups in sheltered, shallow water.

DID YOU KNOW? Swell sharks are named for their ability to gulp in water when frightened, making themselves too big for a predator to swallow.

Together and Apart

Some sharks spend much of their time in a group, usually known as a school or shiver. Other sharks live alone, except when they gather to mate with other sharks of their species. Many sharks travel long distances to reach the same area for each mating season.

In June and July, nurse sharks gather together to mate, returning to the same area every time.

Useful Schools

Many sharks spend time together and time apart. Great hammerheads swim in large schools during the day, but separate at night to hunt. Hunting alone means they do not compete for food. Small-spotted catsharks also hunt alone, but gather together to rest on the seafloor. This gives smaller sharks protection, as there are many eyes to watch for danger. Some sharks, including lemon sharks, do hunt together, helping each other to corner prey. Yet scientists have noticed that some sharks come together for no obvious reason, unless it is for company. Sand tigers are large predators that always return to the same shark "friends" after hunting trips.

Adult oceanic blacktip sharks are usually seen in schools. Pups form their own schools in the shallow waters where they are born.

AGGREGATIONS

Oceanic blacktip sharks: Up to 12,000
Basking sharks: Up to 1,400
Grey reef sharks: Up to 700
Whale sharks: Up to 400
Scalloped hammerheads: Up to 300

Grey reef shark aggregation

Migration and Aggregation

Although some sharks remain in the same area throughout their life, many sharks migrate (travel from one area to another) to reach suitable places to mate, give birth, or feed, gathering there in their tens or hundreds at certain times of year. These large, seasonal groups of sharks are known as aggregations. Some large, fast-swimming sharks, including dusky sharks, migrate to follow the migrations of the fish they prey on. Great white sharks are known to gather at particular beaches when they know that seal pups are born. Scientists believe that sharks know it is time to migrate from changes in water temperature.

Nurse sharks are found in warm, shallow water where mangroves grow.

This male and female shark are courting, or getting to know each other, before mating.

At certain times of year, whale sharks gather in coastal areas where there are plenty of fish eggs.

DID YOU KNOW? For 841 days, scientists tracked a female whale shark who swam a total of 20,142 km (12,516 miles) around the Pacific Ocean.

Under Threat

Around a third of shark species are threatened with extinction. To protect these wonderful fish, some countries have banned or limited shark fishing. There are now many sanctuaries where sharks and their habitats are protected from fishing and pollution.

Sharks in Trouble

Overfishing is the greatest threat faced by sharks. This is when too many fish in a species are caught, leaving the remaining fish unable to have enough babies to keep up their numbers. Sharks are particularly at risk because they do not mature enough to have babies until they are at least 4 years old. Sharks are fished for their meat; their fins, which are used in soup in some regions; and their cartilage and liver oil, which are used in cosmetics. In addition, sharks are often caught in nets and longlines (long cords with many hooks) meant for other fish. Another threat to sharks is water pollution by plastics and industrial chemicals. Construction along coastlines can also damage the shallow-water habitats where some shark pups live.

The oceanic whitetip is critically endangered due to fishing for its fins, meat, liver oil, and skin.

Sharks are sometimes fished for fun, known as sport fishing. However, this spinner shark was returned to the water unharmed. Spinner sharks are ranked as endangered.

DID YOU KNOW? Up to 100 million sharks are killed each year by humans fishing for money or sport.

Known for its white-tipped, rounded fins, this shark swims in the warm waters of the Atlantic, Indian, and Pacific Oceans.

Conservation Status

The scientists of the International Union for Conservation of Nature count and monitor the world's animal species. They classify each species, such as great white shark or tiger shark, by how likely it is to become extinct in the near future:

The tawny nurse shark is ranked as vulnerable due to overfishing and damage to the seagrass meadows and coral reefs of its coastal habitat.

Critically endangered	At extremely high risk of becoming extinct.
Endangered	Very likely to become extinct in the near future.
Vulnerable	Facing a high risk of extinction in the medium term.
Near threatened	Likely to become endangered in the near future.
Least concern	Not currently at risk.

Female oceanic whitetips do not mature until 7 years old, then have only 5 or 6 pups every 2 years.

Sand tiger shark

MOST ENDANGERED

All critically endangered

Pondicherry shark: Coasts and rivers of southern Asia and Australasia
Ganges shark: Coasts and rivers of Bangladesh and India
Sawback angelshark: Coasts of western Africa and southern Europe
Daggernose shark: Coasts of northeastern South America
Sand tiger shark: Coasts of the Americas, Europe, Africa, Asia, and Australasia

Shark Orders

There are over 500 species of sharks, which scientists have divided into eight orders. The sharks in each order share characteristics. The largest order, with 270 species, is the ground sharks. The seven strange species of frilled and cow sharks make up the smallest order.

The great hammerhead is the largest species of hammerhead shark.

The great hammerhead shark is in the Sphyrnidae family of hammerhead sharks, in the ground shark order.

GREAT HAMMERHEAD SHARK

Sphyrna mokarran

Ground shark

Length: 3.5 to 6.1 m (11.5 to 20 ft)
Range: Atlantic, Indian, and Pacific Oceans
Habitat: Coastal tropical and temperate waters to 80 m (260 ft) deep
Diet: Crabs, squid, octopus, and fish including smaller sharks
Conservation: Critically endangered

Scientific Groups

Scientists divide animals into groups, based on how closely the animals are related. Animals in a group are similar in the way they look and behave because they evolved from the same ancestors. Orders are divided into families, which are split into genera, which are split into species. A species is a group of animals that look very alike, share habits, and can make babies together.

Shark Order	Scientific Name	Description	
Ground Sharks	*Carcharhiniformes*	The ground sharks have five gill slits, two dorsal fins, and an anal fin. Their wide, sharp-toothed mouths are located behind their eyes, when viewed from the side. Their eyes are protected by a third, see-through eyelid known as a nictitating membrane.	Silky shark
Carpet Sharks	*Orectolobiformes*	There are around 43 species of carpet sharks, which usually feed on the seabed. They have five gill slits, two dorsal fins, and an anal fin. When viewed from the side, their small mouth does not extend behind their eyes. Many have whisker-like sense organs known as barbels.	Nurse shark
Mackerel Sharks	*Lamniformes*	The 15 species of mackerel sharks have five gill slits, two dorsal fins, and an anal fin. Most species have a long snout and a large mouth that stretches behind their eyes. Most mackerel sharks are large.	Great white shark
Dogfish Sharks	*Squaliformes*	The 126 sharks in this order have five gill slits, two dorsal fins that are usually armed with spines, and no anal fin. They have a short mouth and a fairly pointed snout.	Spiny dogfish
Frilled and Cow Sharks	*Hexanchiformes*	These sharks have six or seven gill slits, one dorsal fin, and an anal fin. Their teeth are thornlike. Most sharks in this order live in cold, deep water. These sharks are similar to extinct sharks known only from fossils.	Broadnose sevengill shark
Bullhead Sharks	*Heterodontiformes*	This order contains nine species of small sharks. They have five gill slits, two dorsal fins armed with sharp spines, and an anal fin. Their mouth contains both sharp and flat teeth. Bullhead sharks feed at the ocean floor in tropical and subtropical oceans.	Port Jackson shark
Sawsharks	*Pristiophoriformes*	The eight species of sawsharks have long, sawlike snouts edged with sharp teeth. A pair of barbels is partway along the snout. Sawsharks have five or six gill slits, two dorsal fins, and no anal fin. These sharks usually live in coastal tropical waters.	Japanese sawshark
Angelsharks	*Squatiniformes*	There are around 24 species of angelsharks. They have five gill slits, two dorsal fins, and no anal fin. They have a flattened body and wide pectoral fins. Their jaws can be extended to give a rapid snap. Angelsharks usually live on sandy, shallow seabeds.	Pacific angelshark

DID YOU KNOW? Carpet sharks are named for their patterned bodies, which look a little like carpet designs.

Scalloped Hammerhead

Like other sharks in the hammerhead family, the scalloped hammerhead has an unusually shaped head, which is extended sideways into a hammer shape. The shark's eyes and nostrils are positioned at the tips of the hammer-like extension, which is known as a cephalofoil.

The front edge of this hammerhead's cephalofoil is scalloped, unlike that of the great hammerhead (see page 26), which is straighter.

There are 17 rows of small, sharp teeth on both the upper and lower jaw.

Helpful Hammer

This shark's head shape is useful for finding prey. Having eyes at either end of its cephalofoil enables the hammerhead to see above and below at all times. Although the shark does have a blind spot in front of its head, it swings its head from side to side as it swims to see what is directly ahead. In addition, the cephalofoil is covered in pores called ampullae of Lorenzini (see page 16), which detect the electrical charges given off by prey. This sense is called electroreception. Since the hammerhead's ampullae cover a wide area, it can even detect prey buried in sand.

SCALLOPED HAMMERHEAD

Sphyrna lewini

Ground shark

Length: 1.5 to 4.3 m (4.9 to 14 ft)
Range: Atlantic, Indian, and Pacific Oceans
Habitat: Coastal tropical and temperate waters to 500 m (1,600 ft) deep
Diet: Fish, squid, and octopus
Conservation: Critically endangered

Along with other sharks in the ground shark order, the scalloped hammerhead has five gill slits.

A school of scalloped hammerheads swims into deeper waters in search of food, but returns to shallower water to mate.

Swimming in a School

Scalloped hammerheads are usually seen in schools of up to several hundred sharks. Swimming in a group offers protection to younger sharks, which stay close to the surface while adults swim deeper. Attacks from larger sharks, such as great whites, will usually be made from below. In addition, scalloped hammerheads often work with members of their school to corner prey.

The black-tipped pectoral fins are held at an angle to help with balance.

DID YOU KNOW? A female scalloped hammerhead gives birth to litters of up to 40 live pups, but most do not survive to adulthood.

Bonnethead

Also known as a shovelhead, the bonnethead is a small member of the hammerhead shark family. It hunts by swinging its shovel-shaped head above the seafloor, trying to detect the tiny electrical charges given off by prey hiding among the mud and seagrass.

The Only Plant-Eater

The bonnethead is the only shark known to eat plants. It eats large amounts of seagrass, which may line its stomach for protection from the spiny shells of the blue crabs this shark also often eats. To crush these shells, the bonnethead has broad, flat teeth at the back of its mouth. It also has small, sharp teeth at the front of the mouth for grabbing little, slippery fish.

A bonnethead smells prey by detecting tiny particles—of blood, mucus, and other materials—that wash off prey and into its nostrils.

More than half a bonnethead's diet is made up of seagrass. Unlike other sharks, its guts make chemicals that can break down tough plant materials.

BONNETHEAD SHARK

Sphyrna tiburo

Ground shark

Length: 0.8 to 1.5 m (2.6 to 4.9 ft)
Range: Coasts of the Americas in the Atlantic and Pacific Oceans
Habitat: Seagrass beds of shallow bays in tropical and temperate waters to 80 m (260 ft) deep
Diet: Seagrass, blue crabs, shrimp, and small fish
Conservation: Endangered

DID YOU KNOW? A female bonnethead gives birth to live pups 5 months after mating, giving her the shortest known shark pregnancy.

This female bonnethead has a straight back to her cephalofoil, while a male bonnethead's cephalofoil has a bulging back.

Steering

Most hammerheads use their wide heads for steering as they swim, a little like a cyclist uses the handlebars to steer their bicycle. Other types of sharks use their pectoral fins for steering, but most hammerheads use them only for balance. The bonnethead has the smallest cephalofoil in the hammerhead family. Due to this small cephalofoil, the bonnethead has larger pectoral fins than other hammerheads and uses them energetically for making turns.

Bonnetheads turn and tilt their pectoral fins to swim up, down, left, and right.

31

Puffadder Shyshark

This small shark spends most of its time lying on the seafloor. Its narrow jaws have around 30 rows of teeth. Males, which prefer to eat worms, have long, three-pointed teeth for grasping. Females, which prey on tougher crabs and shrimp, have shorter, five-pointed teeth for crushing.

Being Shy

The puffadder is one of four species of shysharks. These sharks are named for their posture when they are frightened by a larger shark or other big fish. Shysharks curl into a circle and cover their eyes with their tail. This posture may help a shyshark look like a rock or piece of coral. It also makes the shark more difficult for a predator to swallow.

A pattern of white spots and orange "saddles" provides camouflage among rocks, sand, and coral.

This dark shyshark has curled into its defensive posture.

This puffadder shyshark is lying among Cape sea urchins and starfish in South Africa's False Bay.

DID YOU KNOW? The puffadder shyshark is named for the puff adder snake, which has a similar camouflage pattern.

PUFFADDER SHYSHARK

Haploblepharus edwardsii

Ground shark

Length: 48 to 69 cm (19 to 27 in)
Range: Coast of southern Africa in the Indian Ocean
Habitat: Sandy and rocky seafloors to 130 m (430 ft) deep
Diet: Crabs, shrimp, worms, and small fish
Conservation: Endangered

A puffadder shyshark's eyes are high on the sides of its head, enabling it to watch for danger nearly all around. Behind each eye is a hole known as a spiracle, through which water passes to the gills.

Its rounded pectoral fins and flattened body are suited to slow movement along the seafloor.

Cat Eyes

The shysharks are in the catshark family, in the ground shark order. Catsharks have wide, oval-shaped eyes that resemble a cat's. Their pupils (the holes through which light passes into the eye) are horizontal slits. While this shape would not be helpful for focussing on fast-moving prey, it is useful for watching for predators to the left and right. Like cats, catsharks have a see-through third eyelid, known as a nictitating membrane, that can close to protect the eyeball from damage.

Small-Spotted Catshark

This catshark has a slender body and a rounded snout. It is a slow swimmer that hunts for small prey at night, using stealth rather than speed. Like other catsharks, a female small-spotted catshark lays eggs rather than giving birth to live young.

Egg-Layer

A female lays up to 20 eggs in each mating season. The eggs are protected by a horny case that has curly stringlike tendrils. The female lays her eggs among coral or seaweed, often swimming round and round as she does so until the tendrils tangle on the fronds to stop the egg cases drifting away. The growing baby, known as an embryo, develops inside the egg case for between 5 and 11 months before hatching.

A newborn small-spotted catshark pup is just 10 cm (4 in) long and must hide among the coral for protection.

Inside this newly laid egg case is a yolk sac, which feeds the embryo as it grows.

SMALL-SPOTTED CATSHARK

Scyliorhinus canicula

Ground shark

Length: 0.6 to 1 m (2 to 3.3 ft)
Range: Coasts of Africa and Europe in the Atlantic Ocean
Habitat: Sandy, gravelly, and muddy seabeds to 400 m (1,300 ft) deep
Diet: Crabs, shrimp, fish, worms, and sea squirts
Conservation: Least concern

Researchers have noticed that some small-spotted catsharks prefer to be alone, which suggests that catsharks have different personalities.

Making Choices

This catshark spends the day resting on the seafloor, where it is well camouflaged by its pattern of dark brown spots on sandy skin. Scientists have noticed that some small-spotted catsharks prefer always to lie alone, relying on their own camouflage and stillness for safety. Other small-spotted catsharks always lie in a group, usually on top of each other, so they can share the work of looking out for predators.

A female small-spotted catshark deposited this egg case on a coral called a violescent sea-whip.

The egg case measures around 4 cm (1.6 in) long.

DID YOU KNOW? Young small-spotted catsharks stick prey to the spiky scales near their tail, then tear off bite-sized chunks.

Banded Houndshark

This species is named for the dark stripes along the backs of young banded houndsharks. These stripes fade with age. Banded houndsharks also change their diet as they get older, with young sharks eating shrimp and spoon worms but older sharks eating octopus and crab.

In and Out

Like other sharks, the banded houndshark has two nostrils, called nares, on the underside of its snout. Each nare has two openings, with water flowing in through one opening and out through the other. The banded houndshark has a flap in front of its nares, called a nasal flap, which directs the flow of water in and out of these openings. Inside the nare, the water runs over sensitive cells, which detect chemicals, or "smells," in the water then send signals to the shark's brain.

The banded houndshark has nasal flaps as well as long labial folds, which are furrows of skin around the corners of its mouth.

BANDED HOUNDSHARK

Triakis scyllium

Ground shark

Length: 1 to 1.5 m (3.3 to 5 ft)
Range: Coasts of Asia in the Pacific Ocean
Habitat: Sandy seabeds and seagrass beds in temperate waters to 150 m (490 ft) deep
Diet: Crabs, shrimp, octopus, worms, and fish
Conservation: Endangered

Getting Together

Banded houndsharks are nocturnal. They hunt alone at night, but during the day they may gather in groups on the ocean floor in calm resting areas. Large numbers of houndsharks may also cluster around fishing boats when fish too young to sell are being thrown back into the water.

The back edge of the first dorsal fin is nearly vertical.

Banded houndsharks often rest on sandy seabeds in sheltered bays and estuaries. They can tolerate brackish water, where freshwater and seawater mix to make water that is less salty than seawater.

The banded houndshark's second dorsal fin is three-quarters as tall as the first dorsal fin.

Like all sharks, it has a caudal fin that is heterocercal, which means its upper portion, called a lobe, is bigger than its lower lobe. There is a notch in the upper lobe.

DID YOU KNOW? Female banded houndsharks sometimes produce pups without mating with a male, which is an unusual ability known as parthenogenesis.

Caribbean Reef Shark

This shark is a member of the requiem shark family, in the ground shark order. Requiem sharks are fast and fearsome hunters. Yet Caribbean reef sharks are nicknamed "sleeping sharks" due to their habit of resting inside caves, usually where there are bubbling water currents to massage their skin.

All in the Name

The requiem sharks probably got their name from the French word for shark, *requin*. This word may have developed from the Latin word *requiem*, which means "death," as a result of many sharks' deadly hunting abilities. On the other hand, *requin* may have developed from the medieval French word *reschignier*, which means "to grimace with bared teeth."

A requiem shark's body is shaped like a torpedo (a fast-moving underwater weapon), which means it is long and bulky but slimmer at the snout and tail.

Like other requiem sharks, the Caribbean reef shark has a rounded snout and wide mouth.

DID YOU KNOW? Caribbean reef sharks can push their stomach out through their mouth, inside out, to get rid of parasites and food they cannot digest.

Balancing the Coral Reef

The Caribbean reef shark is the most common shark on the Caribbean Sea's Great Mayan Reef, which stretches along the coasts of Mexico, Belize, Guatemala, and Honduras in Central America. This shark is one of the largest predators on the coral reef, so it has a key role in maintaining the balance of reef life. By eating large numbers of smaller predators, such as yellowtail snappers, the shark prevents them from eating too many small, plant-eating animals. Plant-eaters keep the reef clear of algae, so the coral can survive.

The Great Mayan Reef is home to more than 60 species of hard corals, which are tiny animals that usually live in large groups called colonies. They build reefs by constructing hard skeletons around their soft bodies.

This shark is shy around humans but may bite divers if they block its path to prey.

If it feels threatened, this shark tries to frighten away predators by flapping its pectoral fins, arching its back, and darting in different directions.

CARIBBEAN REEF SHARK

Carcharhinus perezi

Ground shark

Length: 2 to 3 m (6.6 to 9.8 ft)
Range: Coasts of the Americas in the Atlantic Ocean
Habitat: Coral reefs in tropical waters to 30 m (98 ft) deep
Diet: Fish, octopus, squid, and crabs
Conservation: Endangered

Lemon Shark

This requiem shark is named for its yellow-brown skin, which camouflages the shark as it swims over the sandy seafloor. Lemon sharks live in groups, which work together to herd fish along the shoreline so they can be caught more easily.

Pick My Parasites

Lemon sharks hunt by night. During the day, they can often be seen resting on the seafloor. For a lemon shark, staying still takes a little more effort than moving, as—without water flow—it must suck water into its mouth and through its gills to take oxygen from it. However, a benefit to staying still is that fish named remoras can cling to the shark and feed on the irritating parasites that live on its skin. Parasites are small living things that live on or in other animals.

Remoras attach to a lemon shark by pressing their back to the shark's skin. A remora's flat, slatted dorsal fin acts like a sticky sucker.

LEMON SHARK

Negaprion brevirostris

Ground shark

Length: 2.4 to 3.1 m (7.9 to 10.2 ft)
Range: Coasts of the Americas and Africa in the Atlantic and Pacific Oceans
Habitat: Mangroves, river mouths, and bays in tropical and temperate waters to 90 m (295 ft) deep
Diet: Fish, crabs, crayfish, and seabirds
Conservation: Vulnerable

DID YOU KNOW? A lemon shark's large brain is as big in comparison to its body size as a bird's brain, which helps these clever sharks to work together.

A large lemon shark can weigh as much as 184 kg (405 lb), more than two adult men.

Although lemon sharks live along busy coasts, they rarely attack swimmers or surfers.

Lemon sharks form groups with other lemon sharks of a similar size.

Around 60 cm (24 in) long at birth, a lemon shark pup grows around 50 cm (20 in) per year while it stays in its mangrove nursery.

Mangrove Nursery

Female lemon sharks give birth to their pups in sheltered, shallow waters, usually among the roots of mangroves. Mangroves are shrubs and trees that grow in warm, shallow seawater. Abandoned by their mother immediately after birth, pups stay among the mangroves for the first three years of their life. Mangroves offer hiding places as well as a barrier to large predators. The pups form groups with other pups, with one pup often being the leader and the rest following as they search for food together.

Bull Shark

Bull sharks are broader than most requiem sharks. They are named for their similarities to a bull: a stocky body, wide snout, and aggression. These dangerous sharks swim in shallow coastal water as well as in rivers, up to 1,100 km (700 miles) from the ocean.

Bull sharks are rarely seen together, except in late summer when they gather to mate in river mouths.

Attacks on People

Bull sharks are responsible for more attacks on people than any shark apart from the great white and tiger shark. This is partly because bull sharks are found in shallow coastal water where people swim and surf. Bull sharks are also territorial: They live alone and like to defend their area, or territory. Attacks on people are not usually deliberate, as bull sharks hunt in murky water and may bite a moving object simply to find out what it is.

Attacks by bull sharks are very rare. However, shark experts advise swimmers to punch an attacking shark hard in the eyes or gills to frighten it away.

BULL SHARK

Carcharhinus leucas

Ground shark

Length: 2 to 3.5 m (6.6 to 11.5 ft)
Range: Atlantic, Indian, and Pacific Oceans, and rivers in the Americas, Africa, Asia, and Australia
Habitat: Coasts in tropical and temperate waters to 150 m (490 ft) deep, as well as rivers and lakes
Diet: Turtles, birds, dolphins, and fish including other sharks
Conservation: Vulnerable

Bull sharks eat any freshwater or saltwater fish they can find.

Living in Freshwater

The bull shark is one of the few sharks that can live in freshwater. Sharks have salty blood, made by taking in both salt and water from seawater. If most sharks take in freshwater, their blood is soon not salty enough for their organs to survive. Their body takes in extra water in an attempt to gain more salt, resulting in bloating and death. In contrast, when a bull shark swims in freshwater, its kidneys help to keep the right balance of salt and water by recycling the body's salt.

A bull shark lives for around 12 to 20 years.

The bull shark's bite has a force of 5,914 newtons, with 1 newton the force needed to fling an object weighing 1 kg (2.2 lb) a distance of 1 m (3.3 ft) in 1 second.

DID YOU KNOW? A bull shark has 50 rows of teeth, each with 7 needle-like teeth, adding up to around 20,000 over the course of its life.

Tiger Shark

Up to 5.5 m (18 ft) long, the tiger shark is the longest of the requiem sharks. It is a fierce, solitary hunter, able to catch and eat a wider range of prey than any other shark, including hard-shelled sea turtles, fast-swimming dolphins, wriggling sea snakes—and other tiger sharks.

Eyelid for Safety

Like other ground sharks, the tiger shark has a see-through eyelid, known as a nictitating membrane, that can cover the eyeball for protection. When feeding, the shark closes the membrane and opens its jaws at exactly the same moment. The membrane is a thick body tissue covered in tiny scales. Like humans, a shark also has an upper and a lower eyelid, but these lids cannot close entirely over the eye.

The nictitating membrane moves over a tiger shark's eye from the bottom to the top.

The Laysan albatross is a common seabird across the North Pacific Ocean.

TIGER SHARK

Galeocerdo cuvier

Ground shark

Length: 3.3 to 5.5 m (10.8 to 18 ft)
Range: Atlantic, Indian, and Pacific Oceans
Habitat: Tropical and subtropical oceans to 900 m (3,000 ft) deep
Diet: Turtles, birds, dolphins, seals, sea snakes, crabs, and fish including other sharks
Conservation: Near threatened

Slanted for Slicing

A tiger shark's teeth are strong and sharp enough to break the shells of sea turtles, including those of leatherbacks, which reach 2 m (6.6 ft) long. This shark's teeth are short, only around 2.5 cm (1 in) long, but very wide. Each tooth has a slanting, knife-like tip for slicing through prey. On the left side of the mouth, these tips slant to the left, while on the right they slant to the right. This gives the shark extra grip while holding struggling prey. In addition, the tooth bases have jagged edges, which can saw through tough bones and shells.

A tiger shark has 48 slanted front teeth, which are replaced throughout its life.

The tiger shark swims slowly and stealthily toward prey, making a burst of speed at the final moment.

Inside a tiger shark's mouth are 10 openings through which water flows to its gills.

DID YOU KNOW? Tiger sharks will eat almost anything they find in the water, including human garbage such as wheels, bottles, nails, and balls.

Blacktip Reef Shark

This requiem shark can be identified by the black tips on its fins. Although the blacktip reef shark is timid with humans, it has been known to mistakenly nip the legs of people wading through the shallows of the Indian and Pacific Oceans.

Patrolling the Reef

An adult blacktip reef shark remains in one area of a coral reef for many years. This "home" area may be just 0.55 sq km (0.21 sq miles), among the smallest territories of any shark. The shark spends most of its time swimming backward and forward along the reef—until it finds prey. If a blacktip reef shark enters deeper water, it may fall victim to a tiger shark, so it usually remains on ledges of the reef, which offer protection from larger fish.

A blacktip reef shark patrols the edges and ledges of a coral reef through both the day and night.

BLACKTIP REEF SHARK

Carcharhinus melanopterus

Ground shark

Length: 1.5 to 1.8 m (5 to 6 ft)
Range: Coasts of Africa, Asia, and Australasia in the Indian and Pacific Oceans
Habitat: Tropical and subtropical waters to 80 m (260 ft) deep
Diet: Small fish, squid, octopus, and shrimp
Conservation: Vulnerable

DID YOU KNOW? At mating time, male and female blacktip reef sharks "court" each other by swimming one behind the other in curving, circling paths.

Around tropical islands, this shark's tall dorsal fin is a common sight as it cuts through the water surface.

The caudal fin and first dorsal fin are marked with the most noticeable black tips.

The wide pectoral fins curve slightly backward.

A Safe Place

After a pregnancy of 7 to 11 months, a female blacktip reef shark gives birth to 2 to 5 pups in a sandy area close to shore, usually in the same spot where she was born. In this nursery area, the reef forms a barrier against ocean waves, while there is plenty of small prey to eat. Newborn pups are 30 to 50 cm (12 to 20 in) long but able to hunt for themselves. They spend up to 4 years in this warm, shallow water, often barely deep enough to cover their body. Pups usually form groups for protection, darting under rocks and coral when a predator is sensed.

In its nursery area, a pup is protected from sharks and other large fish, but it is at risk from birds—and sometimes from humans.

Whale Shark

The largest of the sharks, the whale shark is harmless to humans —and to all animals larger than around a hand's width across. This shark feeds by filtering tiny creatures from the water. It is a slow swimmer, rarely moving faster than 5 km/h (3 miles per hour).

Tiny Food

Inside a whale shark's huge mouth are 300 rows of very small, useless teeth, which play no part in feeding. Instead, a whale shark has 20 sieve-like filter pads in front of its gills. Water can pass through the pads, but not tiny living things—such as eggs, small fish, and shrimp-like animals called krill—which the shark swallows. The whale shark can feed by swimming forward with its mouth open, so water and food flow inside, which is known as ram feeding. It can also feed by sucking water into its mouth, known as suction feeding.

A whale shark can weigh 15,000 kg (33,000 lb), more than 170 adult men.

A whale shark eats more than 20 kg (45 lb) of tiny living things every day.

WHALE SHARK

Rhincodon typus

Carpet shark

Length: 8 to 18.8 m (26 to 61.7 ft)
Range: Atlantic, Indian, and Pacific Oceans
Habitat: Tropical and temperate waters to 1,900 m (6,200 ft) deep
Diet: Eggs, krill, crab larvae, jellyfish, small fish, and squid
Conservation: Endangered

Huge Fish

The largest known whale sharks measure around 18.8 m (61.7 ft). Females grow more slowly than males but continue growing for much longer. The average female reaches around 14.5 m (48 ft) by the age of 50, which is when she is mature enough to mate. The average male grows to around 9 m (30 ft) long by the age of 30, which is when he is able to mate. Whale sharks are believed to live for between 80 and 130 years.

A whale shark's mouth is up to 1.55 m (5.1 ft) wide.

Like other carpet sharks, the whale shark has patterned dermal denticles.

For protection, the eyeballs are covered in dermal denticles and can also be pulled back into their sockets.

DID YOU KNOW? A whale shark can take in around 6,000 l (1,585 gallons) of water every hour—about 24,000 glasses.

Zebra Shark

During the day, this shark rests on the sandy seafloor between the corals of the reef where it lives. At night, the zebra shark uses its long, flexible body to squeeze into crevices in the reef, where it sucks up hiding prey using its muscly mouth.

Making Friends

Zebra sharks usually live alone, but come together to mate. Before mating, male and female zebra sharks court each other. The male may gently bite the female shark's tail. The pair swim side by side as the male holds on to the female's pectoral fin with his mouth. Female zebra sharks lay eggs, depositing up to 46 egg cases over a 112-day period.

Mature zebra sharks are spotted, while young zebra sharks are striped, a little like a zebra. This young shark's stripes are fading.

A female (at the front) and male zebra shark court each other.

ZEBRA SHARK

Stegostoma tigrinum

Carpet shark

Length: 1.5 to 2.5 m (4.9 to 8.2 ft)
Range: Indian and Pacific Oceans
Habitat: Coral reefs in tropical waters to 60 m (200 ft) deep
Diet: Shellfish, shrimp, small fish, and sea snakes
Conservation: Endangered

DID YOU KNOW? Scientists think the stripes of young zebra sharks make them look like venomous sea snakes, which helps to keep predators away.

Larger than the zebra shark's eye, the spiracle is used for sucking in water when the shark is resting so it can continue to take oxygen.

Swimming Style

This shark's caudal (tail) fin is nearly as long as the rest of its body. Unlike more solid-bodied and short-tailed sharks, such as great whites, the zebra shark swims by making snake-like wiggles of its tail and body. This shark has five deep ridges running along its body, which help water wash quickly over the shark so it is not bashed against coral or rocks by choppy waves.

Each nostril has a barbel, a sense organ that helps with tasting and smelling prey.

In most sharks, tall dorsal fins help with stability, but the zebra shark has low dorsal fins. However, it has deep body ridges and wide pectoral fins to help with balance.

Blind Shark

This shark lives in shallow water close to shore. It is sometimes left stranded in rock pools when the tide goes out. Unusually for a shark, the blind shark can survive up to 18 hours out of water by switching off the brain and body functions that are not essential.

Not Blind

Despite its name, this shark has good eyesight. It got its name from its habit of pulling its eyeballs back into their sockets and shutting its thick lower eyelids if caught by a fisherman. This protects its eyes from injury and from drying out in the air. The blind shark is a night-time hunter. Like many other nocturnal sharks, it makes up for poor visibility by having barbels that help it taste and smell prey.

The blind shark has a very long barbel projecting from each nostril.

Hiding in a Cave

During the day, blind sharks usually hide in small caves or under ledges. If surprised by a human or a predator—such as a larger shark—the blind shark becomes completely motionless or tries to wriggle further into its hiding place.

The blind shark likes rocky habitats with plenty of shelter.

Female blind sharks give birth to as many as eight pups in the summer months.

An adult's brown dermal denticles have a pattern of white spots.

Its mouth is small, but its strong cheek muscles enable it to suck in prey.

BLIND SHARK

Brachaelurus waddi

Carpet shark

Length: 0.6 to 1.2 m (2 to 4 ft)
Range: Eastern coast of Australia in the Pacific Ocean
Habitat: Rocky shorelines, coral reefs, and seagrass beds to 140 m (460 ft) deep
Diet: Small fish, shrimp, crabs, and sea anemones
Conservation: Least concern

DID YOU KNOW? If provoked by a diver, the blind shark can bite then cling hard to their skin with its powerful sucking mouth, making it hard to remove.

Nurse Shark

At night, the nurse shark hunts alone, searching among the sand and mud for small, resting creatures. During the day, this shark lies on the seafloor with its school. No one is sure how it got the name "nurse," but it may be related to the fact that females give birth to live pups.

Suck and Spit

Nurse sharks have a small mouth that creates extremely powerful suction to catch prey. To suck in prey, the shark opens its mouth quickly. Water rushes in to fill the empty space in the jaws, drawing prey with it. If prey is too large, the shark breaks it apart by shaking its head vigorously as it sucks. It also uses a suck and spit action: spitting prey out and sucking it back in again and again until it is torn apart.

The nurse shark's small mouth makes its sucking action very focussed and accurate.

A nurse shark school stays in one small area of coastline, where it has its own preferred resting place.

Slow but Snappy

The nurse shark is slow moving and spends much of the day lying still, along with up to 40 others. This "sleepiness" has led foolish divers to approach the shark, thinking it is harmless. When bothered by a human, this shark will bite, putting it among the top 20 shark species most likely to attack humans. This shark's small teeth mean its bites are not life-threatening.

DID YOU KNOW? The nurse shark preys on sea snails by flipping over their shell then sucking out their soft body.

NURSE SHARK

Ginglymostoma cirratum

Carpet shark

Length: 2.1 to 3 m (6.9 to 9.8 ft)
Range: Coasts of the Americas and Africa in the Atlantic and Pacific Oceans
Habitat: Coral reefs and rocky areas in tropical and subtropical waters to 75 m (246 ft) deep
Diet: Fish, octopus, squid, lobsters, sea urchins, clams, and snails
Conservation: Vulnerable

These nurse sharks are swimming among staghorn, fire, and elkhorn corals off the coast of Belize, in Central America.

The nurse shark's two dorsal fins are rounded, with the first located above the pelvic fins.

Its snout is broad and rounded. Inside the mouth are many small, notched teeth for crushing hard-shelled prey.

Brownbanded Bamboo Shark

This long-bodied shark is often found on the sheltered, muddy seafloor between coral reefs and the shore. It hunts at night, by nosing into mud, sand, crevices, and rock pools while using its sensitive barbels to find small creatures.

The brownbanded bamboo shark is listed as near threatened due to fishing, pollution, and damage to its coral reef habitat.

Changing Patterns

Young bamboo sharks have dark-brown bands running around their pale-brown body, earning this species its name. These bands help to camouflage pups, which spend the day hiding among the dappled light and shadows around seagrass, rocks, and coral. The bands fade as the sharks reach maturity, leaving adults a uniform light brown that serves as good camouflage on the seafloor.

A young brownbanded bamboo shark hides from predators such as lemon sharks and killer whales.

Its short barbels help with tasting and smelling prey that is hidden under mud or sand.

BROWNBANDED BAMBOO SHARK

Chiloscyllium punctatum

Carpet shark

Length: 0.8 to 1.3 m (2.6 to 4.3 ft)
Range: Coasts of Asia and Australasia in the Indian and Pacific Oceans
Habitat: Muddy seafloors in tropical and subtropical waters to 85 m (279 ft) deep
Diet: Small fish, shrimp, crabs, and worms
Conservation: Near threatened

Bamboo Sharks

This shark is in the bamboo shark family, also known as longtail carpet sharks. They are named for their long body and extremely lengthy tail, which make them look a little like a bamboo stem. Bamboo sharks have two dorsal fins positioned far back on their body, with the first dorsal fin over their pelvic fin. All bamboo sharks live on the seafloor in shallow waters of the Indian and Pacific Oceans.

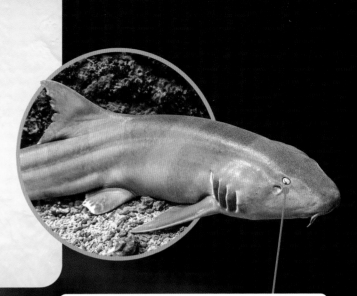

Bamboo sharks have pupils that narrow to vertical slits. This type of pupil is useful in the constantly changing light of shallow water as it enables the pupil to narrow quickly in sudden sunlight to moderate the amount of light entering the eye.

Parasites (which live in or on other living things) are found in this shark's gills, where they feed on blood and mucus.

DID YOU KNOW? When this shark bites hard-shelled prey, its small, sharp teeth fold backward so they can crush the shell with their strong, flat fronts.

Epaulette Shark

This member of the bamboo shark family takes its name from the white-edged, dark spot behind each pectoral fin. These spots look rather like the shoulder ornaments, known as epaulettes, that are sometimes worn by soldiers.

This shark can survive for 2 hours out of water, by increasing the blood supply to its brain to keep it fed with oxygen.

Its large nostrils, or nares, are nearly at the tip of its snout.

Walking Along

Like other members of its family, the epaulette shark lives on the sandy, muddy, or rocky seafloor. Rather than swimming along, it often "walks" across the bottom. It does this by wriggling its body and pushing off the floor with its paddle-shaped pectoral and pelvic fins. This means the shark can move through water too shallow for swimming. It is even able to walk out of the water to reach isolated rock pools where it can find many small, trapped creatures.

The epaulette shark's pectoral and pelvic fins are broad, muscly, and capable of wider movements than those of most other sharks.

This shark's predators include fish such as larger sharks and groupers.

A Frightening Eye

This shark's white-and-black epaulette is known as an eyespot, a marking that resembles an eye. This type of marking is found in animals from butterflies to birds. The eyespot may frighten away predators as it seems to be a huge eye that belongs to a much bigger animal. The marking may also distract predators into attacking the shark's side rather than its sensitive and vital head.

EPAULETTE SHARK

*Hemiscyllium
ocellatum*

Carpet shark

Length: 0.7 to 1 m (2.3 to 3.3 ft)
Range: Coasts of New Guinea and Australia in the Indian and Pacific Oceans
Habitat: Coral reefs and rock pools in tropical waters to 50 m (160 ft) deep
Diet: Worms, crabs, small fish, and shrimp
Conservation: Least concern

Like many sharks that live on the seafloor, the epaulette shark has eyes positioned near the top of its head so it can look upward.

DID YOU KNOW? Unlike most sharks, the epaulette shark sometimes chews food for up to 10 minutes so it can crush shells and bones.

Indonesian Speckled Shark

This little-known shark is found only in one small region, around the coasts and islands of West Papua, in Indonesia. Like other bamboo sharks, its body and fin shapes are suited to slow swimming and crawling along the seafloor and into holes in rocks and reefs.

Diamond-shaped, extra-thick dermal denticles do not help this shark swim faster but do give protection as it rubs against rough coral and rocks.

Bamboo Eggs

Like other bamboo sharks, this shark is an egg-layer. After a female bamboo shark has reached around the age of seven, she lays a pair of eggs every couple of weeks during the mating season. She produces around 50 eggs in a year, always laying them among the shadows under overhanging coral. The babies spend 4 to 5 months developing inside their egg case before hatching. Pups are less than 19 cm (7.5 in) long at birth.

About 10 cm (4 in) long, the egg case of a bamboo shark is very strong. Like the egg cases of other sharks, it is made of strands of collagen, a material also found in human cartilage, bones, and skin.

INDONESIAN SPECKLED CARPET SHARK

Hemiscyllium freycineti

Carpet shark

Length: 37 to 72 cm (15 to 28 in)
Range: Coasts of western New Guinea in the Pacific Ocean
Habitat: Coral reefs, rock pools, and seagrass meadows in tropical waters to 12 m (39 ft) deep
Diet: Worms, crabs, shrimp, and small fish
Conservation: Near threatened

DID YOU KNOW? This shark's scientific name, *Hemiscyllium freycineti*, means "half-dogfish of Freycinet," after the 19th-century explorer who first studied it.

Humans have a white coating to their eye, known as the sclera, but a shark's sclera is protected by a thick body tissue containing cartilage.

Like other members of its family, the Indonesian speckled carpet shark has a large spiracle.

During the day, the Indonesian speckled carpet shark hides in crevices on the coral reef.

Shallow Habitat

This shark lives in shallow, near-shore habitats, where its speckled dermal denticles are effective camouflage, helping to break up the shark's outline as it lies among the dappled light and waving plants. Yet its habitats are under threat from fishing practices such as using dynamite to create explosions that kill both fish and coral.

Tasselled Wobbegong

This shark belongs to the wobbegong family of well-camouflaged carpet sharks, which spend most of their time lying on the seafloor or coral. "Wobbegong" comes from Aboriginal Australian words that may mean "shaggy beard," due to these sharks' tassel-like skin flaps.

Tasty Tassels

This wobbegong has a fringe of branching skin flaps that runs from its snout to its pectoral fins. Looking like seaweed or coral, these flaps camouflage the wobbegong while also attracting small prey to feed on them. When prey animals try to take a nibble, the wobbegong sucks them into its wide mouth, then pierces them with its needle-like teeth. The skin flaps also have sensitive cells that help the wobbegong smell and taste prey.

The tasselled wobbegong is usually an ambush predator, lying in wait for prey then making a sudden, deadly movement.

The wobbegong's flattened, patterned body keeps it camouflaged on the coral reef so unsuspecting prey swims near.

TASSELLED WOBBEGONG

Eucrossorhinus dasypogon

Carpet shark

Length: 1.2 to 1.8 m (3.9 to 5.9 ft)
Range: Coasts of New Guinea and northern Australia in the Indian and Pacific Oceans
Habitat: Coral reefs in tropical waters to 50 m (160 ft) deep
Diet: Fish, squid, shrimp, octopus, and squid
Conservation: Least concern

DID YOU KNOW? The tasselled wobbegong kills sharks almost as big as itself, including brownbanded bamboo sharks.

Fishy Tail

While the tasselled wobbegong waits for prey, it often waves its tail back and forth over its own head, making a slow movement like a small, swimming fish. The tail is also shaped rather like a fish, complete with a dark eyespot at its base. When larger fish approach to snatch the supposed fish, they are caught by the wobbegong instead.

When waving its tail, the wobbegong rests with its head tilted upward, putting its mouth within sucking distance of any animal that takes the bait.

The shark uses its broad, curved pectoral fins for pulling itself over the reef.

While resting during the daytime, this shark will seize prey that comes near, but it does move in search of food at night.

Ornate Wobbegong

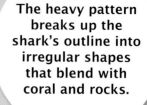

The heavy pattern breaks up the shark's outline into irregular shapes that blend with coral and rocks.

This shark is named for its busy, lace-like pattern of golden brown, cream, and blue-beige. Its underside is yellowish green. This gorgeous pattern provides good camouflage among the corals and seaweeds of the ornate wobbegong's coral reef home.

Mega Mouth

Wobbegongs suck in prey by shooting forward their jaws while expanding their throat and mouth with powerful muscles. Water and prey are sucked in to fill the huge empty space in the mouth. Small prey is swallowed without chewing. If wobbegongs catch an animal too large to swallow, they hold it in their jaws until it dies from exhaustion or lack of oxygen, then bite off chunks with their long, sharp teeth.

Bumps above the shark's eyes keep them hidden in shadow so they do not attract attention.

An ornate wobbegong can open its mouth wide enough to prey on fish as large as a green moray, which reaches 2.5 m (8.2 ft) long when fully grown.

ORNATE WOBBEGONG

Orectolobus ornatus

Carpet shark

Length: 1.7 to 2.9 m (5.6 to 9.5 ft)
Range: Eastern coast of Australia in the Pacific Ocean
Habitat: Coral reefs and algae–covered seafloor in tropical to temperate waters to 100 m (330 ft) deep
Diet: Fish, crabs, lobsters, and octopus
Conservation: Least concern

Looking Up

Like other wobbegongs, the ornate wobbegong has eyes positioned at the top of its head, which lets this bottom-dweller get a wide view of approaching prey and predators. Unlike most sharks, which do not have fully closing eyelids, wobbegongs have more moveable upper and lower eyelids that cover the eyeballs when the shark is pressing its snout into sand or coral in search of prey.

The tissue surrounding the ornate wobbegong's pupil, known as the sclera, is yellow. This helps the shark maintain camouflage.

Like other wobbegongs, this shark has two dorsal fins on the back half of its body, behind its pelvic fins.

DID YOU KNOW? This shark is known to lie in rock pools, where it can give painful bites to humans who accidentally step too close.

65

Necklace Carpet Shark

A member of the collared carpet shark family, this shark is named for the dark, necklace-like patch that lies behind its eyes. Entirely harmless to humans, this small shark has a long, slim body.

Hiding Away

The necklace carpet shark spends its days hidden in caves or on the seafloor, where it shelters from predators among coral, kelp, and seagrass. At night, it uses its barbels and electroreception (see page 16) to smell and sense the movements of small creatures that are hiding among the coral or in the sand.

This shark can be told apart from other members of its family by the small, pale spots on its collar and the large, dark spots on its pectoral fins.

Seafloor Mimic

Scientists think that collared carpet sharks can change the shade of their skin to better match the seafloor on which they are lying. The change takes several minutes, with the shark becoming darker, lighter, or more blotchy. These changes are triggered by the shark's brain releasing a hormone (a chemical that carries messages) which causes melanophores in the skin to expand or contract. Melanophores are cells that are filled with a dark pigment, named melanin.

The necklace carpet shark's dark collar helps with camouflage by breaking up the shark's outline.

NECKLACE CARPET SHARK

Parascyllium variolatum

Carpet shark

Length: 60 to 91 cm (24 to 36 in)
Range: Southern coast of Australia in the Indian and Pacific Oceans
Habitat: Coral reefs, kelp forest, and seagrass meadows in temperate waters to 180 m (590 ft) deep
Diet: Prawns, shrimp, and crabs
Conservation: Least concern

This shark's pupils narrow to horizontal slits, a shape that gives a wide field of vision and is useful for watching out for predators.

The necklace carpet shark's collar may help other members of its species to recognize it at mating time.

A pair of barbels is used for smelling and tasting prey.

DID YOU KNOW? Two unknown species of collared carpet sharks have been found since the start of the 21st century: the ginger and elongate carpet sharks.

67

Great White Shark

Reaching 6.1 m (20 ft) long, this feared hunter is the world's largest predatory fish. It is responsible for more bites to humans than any other shark. The great white is in the order of mackerel sharks, which are known for their large mouth and wide-opening jaws.

Apex Predator

The great white shark is an apex predator (or "top hunter"), which means that—unless it is young or sick—it is rarely preyed on by other animals. With its powerful, smoothly shaped body and strong jaws, a great white can attack prey as big as a killer whale. Although the great white usually hunts alone, it may work with other members of its school, which can include two or more sharks. When attacking, a great white swims slowly closer to its prey, then makes a sudden rush at up to 24 km/h (15 miles per hour).

The great white shark's first dorsal fin is large and triangular.

A great white has up to 300 jagged-edged, triangular teeth in seven rows. When teeth in the front row break, the teeth behind move forward.

GREAT WHITE SHARK

Carcharodon carcharias

Mackerel shark

Length: 3.4 to 6.1 m (11 to 20 ft)
Range: Atlantic, Indian, and Pacific Oceans
Habitat: Coastal and offshore waters to 1,200 m (3,900 ft) deep
Diet: Fish, dolphins, whales, seals, sea lions, sea turtles, and seabirds
Conservation: Vulnerable

Clever Camouflage

A great white's underside is white, but its back is dark. This pattern is a form of camouflage known as countershading. Such shading makes it difficult for prey swimming at the water surface to see a great white as it moves through the dark water below. Yet for prey swimming below a great white, the shark's pale belly makes it hard to spot against the sunlight shining down through the water.

Like all mackerel sharks, a great white has five gill slits.

A great white shark's most powerful sense is smell: It can smell a drop of blood in 10 billion drops of water.

Great whites attack prey on the water surface by making a sudden upward rush, launching both shark and prey out of the water.

DID YOU KNOW? At the moment when it attacks prey, a great white's eyeballs roll backward in their sockets for protection.

Shortfin Mako Shark

A close relative of the great white shark, the shortfin mako is the fastest known shark. Its smoothly shaped, muscly body and pointed snout let it cut through the water at high speed, reaching 74 km/h (46 miles per hour) in the moments before it seizes prey.

Nicely Named

In the Māori language of New Zealand, mako means "shark" or "shark tooth." In the past, Māori craftspeople carved necklaces from shark teeth, which were believed to give the wearer the strength and ferocity of a shark. The mako is also known as the blue pointer, due to the metallic blue of its back. This shade makes the shark blend with the water, when viewed from above. Yet the shark's underside is white, so that—when seen from below—it is difficult to spot when sunlight is shining down through the water.

The shortfin mako has shorter pectoral fins than its close relative, the longfin mako shark.

SHORTFIN MAKO SHARK

Isurus oxyrinchus

Mackerel shark

Length: 3 to 4 m (9.8 to 13 ft)
Range: Atlantic, Indian, and Pacific Oceans
Habitat: Open ocean in tropical and temperate waters to 150 m (490 ft) deep
Diet: Fish, octopus, squid, porpoises, turtles, and birds
Conservation: Endangered

DID YOU KNOW? The shortfin mako has the strongest recorded bite of any shark, inflicting the same force as a weight of 1,360 kg (3,000 lb).

Hooked Teeth

The shortfin mako shark has very sharp, pointed teeth up to 2 cm (0.8 in) long. The teeth are curved into a hook shape. Such teeth are ideal for piercing and holding on to large, fast-swimming fish, such as tuna, swordfish, and other sharks. Tuna are among the quickest fish, reaching speeds of up to 75 km/h (47 miles per hour). After this shark grasps fish, they are swallowed whole, then digested in the mako's stomach for around 2 days.

When prey such as porpoises or sharks is too large to swallow, the shortfin mako bites chunks out of them.

The shortfin mako shark has extremely large eyes that help it see during deep-water dives.

This shark is a lone hunter, swimming up to 2,000 km (1,240 miles) a month as it follows schools of fish.

The shortfin mako shark usually rests near the water surface at night.

Porbeagle

The porbeagle spends part of its time alone and part with its school, when it has been seen chasing other members of its group in play. That makes this intelligent fish one of the few sharks that is known to play.

This shark's first dorsal fin and pectoral fins are large, but it has very small second dorsal, anal, and pelvic fins.

Watching the Porbeagle

The porbeagle is ranked as vulnerable due to decades of overfishing. Today, many countries have banned or limited the catching of porbeagles. Conservationists monitor this shark's numbers and movements so that more controls can be put in place if needed. Sharks are fitted with telemetry (meaning "distant measuring") tags that record their location, depth, speed, and temperature. The information is sent as radio waves or sound waves to a satellite or underwater receiver, from which it is transmitted to a conservationist's computer.

Captured off the Canadian coast, this porbeagle is being measured and tagged before being released unharmed back into the water. If the shark is caught again, it will be remeasured to discover its growth.

The porbeagle has 26 to 29 front teeth in its lower jaw, with wide gaps between each tooth.

72

Big Black Eyes

The porbeagle's eyes are very large, a feature that lets as much light as possible enter its pupils so it can see when diving deep. In bright, surface conditions, the shark's pupils narrow to a slit so the shark is not dazzled. Like other mackerel sharks, the porbeagle does not have a see-through third eyelid, known as a nictitating membrane, which helps some sharks to protect their eyeballs. Instead, it may roll its eyeballs backward when attacking.

The porbeagle's pupils are surrounded by dark tissue, making the eye look entirely black.

Like the great white, mako, and salmon sharks, it has extremely long gill slits, which help it take in lots of oxygen to fuel its muscles and brain.

PORBEAGLE

Lamna nasus

Mackerel shark

Length: 2 to 3.5 m (6.6 to 11.5 ft)
Range: Atlantic, Indian, Pacific, and Arctic Oceans
Habitat: Open ocean in temperate waters to 1,360 m (4,460 ft) deep
Diet: Fish, squid, and octopus
Conservation: Vulnerable

DID YOU KNOW? Porbeagles give birth to live pups, which feed on unused eggs while they grow inside their mother, a practice known as oophagy ("egg-eating").

Salmon Shark

The majority of sharks live in warm water, but the salmon shark lives in the cool North Pacific Ocean. For most of the year, male and female salmon sharks swim in separate groups, with females usually in the northeastern Pacific and most males in the northwestern Pacific.

Salmon-Eater

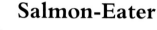

The salmon shark is named for its main prey: salmon. From July to September, these sharks gather in a large aggregation in Alaska's Prince William Sound. Here they catch salmon that are migrating from the ocean to the rivers where they lay their eggs. In addition, salmon sharks eat other large fish, such as cod, herring, and sablefish, as well as most prey they can fit in their mouth.

Scientists estimate that, every year, salmon sharks catch between 76 and 146 million salmon in Prince William Sound.

Warm-Blooded

Most sharks, like most fish, are cold-blooded, which means the temperature of their body is the same as the water around them. Five species of closely related mackerel sharks—the salmon, great white, shortfin mako, longfin mako, and porbeagle sharks—are warm-blooded. This means they can raise their body temperature above the temperature of the surrounding water. They can do this thanks to a complex system of blood vessels, which keeps the heat given off by their muscles as they work. In addition, these sharks' higher body heat keeps their muscles warm. Warmer muscles are able to move faster, giving them an advantage over the cold-blooded fish they prey on.

The salmon shark is the most warm-blooded shark, able to keep its body temperature up to 15.6 °C (60.1 °F) higher than the cool waters where it lives.

SALMON SHARK

Lamna ditropis

Mackerel shark

Length: 2 to 3 m (6.6 to 9.8 ft)
Range: North Pacific Ocean
Habitat: Temperate and polar waters to 668 m (2,192 ft) deep
Diet: Fish, sea otters, and birds
Conservation: Least concern

Copepod parasites are trailing from this shark's first dorsal fin, where they feed on skin and blood.

This salmon shark is cruising in Alaska's Prince William Sound, in the northwestern United States.

Its eyes are positioned toward the front of its head, so the two eyes can work together to judge the distance to fleeing prey.

DID YOU KNOW? The average salmon shark eats around 5 kg (11 lb) of food every day, about the weight of a 2-month-old baby.

Sand Tiger Shark

This shark is named for its habit of hunting in shallow water, often among the breaking waves on sandy beaches. The sand tiger hunts at night, sometimes feeding on large schools of fish alongside other members of its group.

This species can be recognized by the reddish spots on its upper side.

Gulping Air

Sharks are heavier than water, so they sink slowly if they do not swim (see page 14). The sand tiger has a unique answer to this problem: It swims to the surface and gulps air into its stomach, which has the same effect as putting on an air-filled float vest. This habit lets the sand tiger float in the water without moving or making a noise. It is able to surprise passing fish, snatching them up with a sudden sideways snap.

A sand tiger kills prey up to half its own length, using its long, sharp teeth to bite prey into three or four easy-to-swallow chunks.

SAND TIGER SHARK

Carcharias taurus

Mackerel shark

Length: 2 to 3.2 m (6.6 to 10.5 ft)
Range: Atlantic, Indian, and Pacific Oceans
Habitat: Sandy coasts and coral reefs in tropical and temperate waters to 190 m (623 ft) deep
Diet: Fish including small sharks
Conservation: Critically endangered

DID YOU KNOW? This overfished shark is critically endangered due to mothers having only two pups at a time, in every second or third year.

The sand tiger has a long, cone-shaped snout.

It usually swims with its mouth open, revealing its curving teeth—and earning itself the alternative name of "spotted ragged-tooth shark."

This female sand tiger is pregnant.

Cannibal Babies

Female sand tigers give birth to live pups. Females have two areas, called horns, in their uterus. The uterus is a stretchy organ where unborn babies, known as embryos, develop. At the start of a pregnancy, each horn has up to 50 embryos. When one of the embryos reaches 10 cm (4 in) long, it eats all the smaller embryos in its horn. This practice, known as embryophagy (meaning "embryo-eating"), ensures that only large, strong pups are born. The two remaining embryos then eat any unused eggs. After a pregnancy of 8 to 9 months, the mother gives birth to two pups around 1 m (3.3 ft) long.

Smalltooth Sand Tiger Shark

Little is known about the habits of this rarely seen shark, which spends most of its time in rocky, deep-water habitats. It has been seen around ridges and mountains on the ocean floor, as well as hydrothermal vents, where water heated inside the Earth bubbles up.

Small Teeth

The smalltooth sand tiger looks similar to the sand tiger shark, although it is not much more closely related to it than to other mackerel sharks. The smalltooth has smaller teeth than its lookalike. While the sand tiger has sharp front teeth suited to cutting and broader back teeth suited to crushing, the smalltooth's teeth are all alike. This suggests it eats smaller, easier-to-chew prey.

The smalltooth sand tiger has 48 to 56 front teeth in its upper jaw and 36 to 46 front teeth in its lower jaw.

Shark Gods

The smalltooth sand tiger can be spotted around Pacific Islands, where sharks are important characters in myths. For many centuries, people on these islands lived by fishing aboard small boats, with sharks both the most prized catch and the most feared danger. In Hawaiian mythology, Kamohoali'i was a shark god, believed to help ships lost at sea by shaking his tail in front of the ship and then leading the way home.

In Fiji, the shark god Dakuwaqa protected fishermen at sea. The god could take any form he liked, but was often carved as a fierce-looking warrior.

Despite the smalltooth sand tiger's size and fierce appearance, it is gentle toward divers.

The caudal fin has a much larger upper lobe than lower lobe, making it highly asymmetrical.

The large, triangular anal fin is almost the same size as the second dorsal fin.

SMALLTOOTH SAND TIGER SHARK

Odontaspis ferox

Mackerel shark

Length: 3.6 to 4.5 m (11.8 to 14.8 ft)
Range: Atlantic, Indian, and Pacific Oceans
Habitat: Rocky seafloors, coral reefs, and sandy coasts in tropical waters to 2,000 m (6,562 ft) deep
Diet: Fish, squid, and shrimp
Conservation: Vulnerable

DID YOU KNOW? When frightened, this shark stops, opens its mouth, turns around, then shakes its tail toward the threat.

Megamouth Shark

Like the basking and whale sharks, the megamouth is a filter feeder. It eats small animals that it filters from the water by swimming with its mouth open or by sucking in water. Tiny animals are caught on sieve-like bristles in its mouth, while the water flows out of its gills.

Up and Down

The megamouth follows the daily movements of the zooplankton (tiny animals) that it eats. During the day, the shark swims in the murky depths. As night falls, zooplankton including shrimp and krill swim from the depths to the surface to feed on phytoplankton in the safety of darkness. Phytoplankton are tiny, plantlike living things that float near the surface, where they make their own food from sunlight during the day. The megamouth swims upward with the shrimp and krill, spending the night at a depth of around 12 to 25 m (39 to 82 ft).

The megamouth's daily movement between upper and lower waters is known as a diel vertical migration (diel means "daily").

As its name suggests, the megamouth shark has a huge mouth, up to 1.3 m (4.3 ft) wide, so it can take in big mouthfuls of water.

DID YOU KNOW? Since the megamouth shark was discovered in 1976, only around 100 of these rare sharks have been spotted.

An Attractive Lip

When the megamouth's mouth is open, its upper lip is visible and shines a bright silvery white. After the megamouth was first discovered, scientists thought its lip had special light-making cells. Today, scientists think the lip does not make light but does reflect a lot of light. It is covered with guanine crystals, the same material that makes fish scales shiny. The bright shine of the lip attracts small animals, which are then sucked into the shark's mouth.

Scars on the shark's skin were probably gained from collisions with boats or from wrestling with other sharks during mating.

Small ocean animals are attracted to light because they link light with food, due to the fact that sunlit surface waters are rich with food.

The megamouth weighs up to 1,215 kg (2,679 lb), more than 15 adult men.

MEGAMOUTH SHARK

Megachasma pelagios

Mackerel shark

Length: 3.8 to 5.5 m (12.5 to 18 ft)
Range: Atlantic, Indian, and Pacific Oceans
Habitat: Open ocean in tropical and temperate waters to 1,000 m (3,280 ft) deep
Diet: Krill, shrimp, copepods, and jellyfish
Conservation: Least concern

Basking Shark

This filter feeder is the second largest shark, after the whale shark. It is named for its habit of swimming near the zooplankton-filled water surface, giving the mistaken idea that it is basking—or warming itself in the sunshine.

A Simple Life

Of all the sharks, the basking shark has the lightest brain compared to its body weight. Little brain power is needed for this shark's slow and simple lifestyle. Unlike the megamouth and whale sharks, this shark never sucks water into its mouth, but only feeds by swimming with its mouth open, at around 3.7 km/h (2.3 miles per hour). Due to the basking shark's great size, it has little need to use brain power for escaping from predators.

It has 1,500 teeth, each around 0.5 cm (0.2 in) long, which are not used for feeding but are "leftovers" from long–ago ancestors that did bite prey.

On each side of the basking shark's mouth are five openings to its gills, known as gill arches. Each arch is lined with dark, bristly gill rakers that stop tiny animals from entering the gills—directing them toward the shark's throat instead. The gill rakers become so worn with use that they are shed and regrown around once a year.

BASKING SHARK

Cetorhinus maximus

Mackerel shark

Length: 7 to 12.3 m (23 to 40.3 ft)
Range: Atlantic, Indian, Pacific, and Arctic Oceans
Habitat: Temperate and polar waters to 910 m (2,990 ft) deep
Diet: Copepods, fish eggs, and worms
Conservation: Endangered

This basking shark is feeding around St Michael's Mount, in England's Cornwall.

Every 2 to 3 minutes, the basking shark flutters its gills to shake trapped food from its gill rakers.

Giant Gills

The basking shark's gill slits nearly encircle its head, making them the largest slits of any shark. These huge openings let around 1,360,000 l (360,000 gallons) of water pass through the gills every hour. To ensure this water contains enough zooplankton to power the basking shark's giant body, these sharks migrate across the ocean to find areas where weather and currents combine to create clouds of zooplankton.

The basking shark usually swims alone, but in summer may gather in aggregations of up to 1,400 in water that is thick with zooplankton.

DID YOU KNOW? A quarter of this shark's weight is its immense liver, which is filled with lighter-than-water oil and helps the shark float with little effort.

Pelagic Thresher

Like other members of the thresher shark family, this shark has a caudal (tail) fin with an exceptionally long upper lobe. Measuring up to 1.5 m (4.9 ft), the tail makes up nearly half the shark's length. The upper lobe is shaped like a thresher, a curved farming tool used to cut crops.

Thrashing Tail

The pelagic thresher hunts in the ocean's twilight zone, around 200 m (660 ft) below the surface, where there is little sunlight. When this shark finds a school of small fish, it circles them to drive the fish into a ball. Then the shark swims swiftly toward the ball, swinging its tail forward over its head so the fish are whipped by the long upper lobe. The slapped, stunned fish are easily snapped up in the shark's jaws.

The pelagic thresher has around 21 small, sharp front teeth in both its upper and lower jaws, with between 5 and 11 rows of replacement teeth behind.

This shark's smoothly shaped body and powerful tail enable it to swim at well over 30 km/h (18 miles per hour).

The pelagic thresher uses its tail as a deadly weapon.

DID YOU KNOW? Pelagic means "living in the open ocean" and comes from the ancient Greek word for wide ocean far from land.

Overfishing

The pelagic thresher is endangered due to overfishing for its meat, fins, skin, and oil. It is also popular with sport fishermen due to its exciting speed and its habit of leaping out of the water, flicking its tail to push itself higher. The shark may jump from the water, known as breaching, to knock parasites off its skin as it slaps back down.

Its large, round eyes help this shark to see prey in deep, dim water.

As well as being fished deliberately, the pelagic thresher is caught accidentally in longlines and nets, often trapped by its own long tail.

PELAGIC THRESHER

Alopias pelagicus

Mackerel shark

Length: 2.6 to 4.3 m (8.5 to 14 ft)
Range: Indian and Pacific Oceans
Habitat: Open ocean in tropical waters to 250 m (820 ft) deep
Diet: Fish, shrimp, and squid
Conservation: Endangered

Goblin Shark

This strange, deep-water shark is extremely rare, although it is not considered endangered because it is not often caught in nets. The goblin shark lives in coastal waters but swims near the ocean floor, so it is never spotted by swimmers.

Its skin has a pinkish tint due to being quite see-through, letting us see blood vessels beneath the skin.

Scary Snout

The goblin shark is named for its long, flat snout, which looks like the long nose of a nasty, monstrous creature in a fairy tale. Some scientists have wondered if the shark uses its snout to stir up the mud and sand of the seafloor to find small prey, but others think the snout is too soft for this use. However, the snout is covered in many ampullae of Lorenzini (see page 16), which can detect the tiny electric fields given off by prey as they move.

The body is not well muscled, making this shark a slow swimmer that must creep up on prey, then use its speedy jaw for surprise.

The goblin shark's snout is used to detect the movement of small creatures in the dark water or hiding in the sand.

GOBLIN SHARK

Mitsukurina owstoni

Mackerel shark

Length: 3 to 6 m (9.8 to 19.7 ft)
Range: Atlantic, Indian, and Pacific Oceans
Habitat: Coastal tropical and temperate waters to 1,370 m (4,490 ft) deep
Diet: Fish, squid, and shrimp
Conservation: Least concern

The goblin shark's jaws spring forward at up to 3.14 m/s (10.3 ft per second). The shark has nail-like teeth with 35 to 53 front teeth in the upper jaw and 31 to 62 front teeth in the lower jaw.

Catapulting Jaw

When the goblin shark finds prey, it shoots its jaws forward and upward. At other times, the jaws are held back by stretchy tissues named ligaments. When the shark relaxes these ligaments, the effect is like releasing the elastic on a catapult. At the same time, the floor of the shark's mouth drops, expanding the space in the mouth so that water and prey are sucked inside.

The fins are small and soft, preventing this shark from making quick changes of direction.

DID YOU KNOW? Discovered near Japan in 1898, the goblin shark is named *tenguzame* in Japanese, after the *tengu*, a mythical creature with a long nose.

87

Greenland Shark

The largest shark in the dogfish shark order, the Greenland shark can weigh over 1,400 kg (3,100 lb). It is also the longest-living of all sharks, able to survive for over 270 years and possibly as many as 500 years.

Cold and Slow

The Greenland shark is the only shark that can live in Arctic waters year round, swimming in water between -2 and 7 °C (28.4 and 44.6 °F). Like most sharks, its body cannot warm itself, so its temperature matches the cold water. A cold body works more slowly, so the shark's heart beats only once every 12 seconds. This shark also moves very slowly, with an average speed of only 1.22 km/h (0.76 miles per hour). Scientists think the shark's slow-working body is linked with its extremely long life.

A parasite named *Ommatokoita* is attached to this shark's eye. Almost blinded, the shark must rely on its excellent senses of smell and hearing.

The Greenland shark waits near holes in the Arctic sea ice to catch seals that are coming up for air.

DID YOU KNOW? Growing by only 0.5 to 1 cm (0.2 to 0.4 in) a year, Greenland sharks do not mature enough to have babies until they are around 150 years old.

Kæstur hákarl is dried in the open air. Around 100 Greenland sharks are caught deliberately every year, while around 3,500 more are caught accidentally in nets meant for fish such as halibut.

Poisonous Flesh

The Greenland shark's flesh contains the chemical trimethylamine oxide, which is made by the shark's body to stabilize its processes in the extremely cold and often deep water where it lives. This chemical also makes the shark poisonous, but in Iceland its flesh is a traditional delicacy known as *kæstur hákarl*. To make the flesh safe to eat, it is buried in the ground for 6 to 12 weeks to press out the trimethylamine oxide, then hung in strips to dry for several months.

With its small pectoral fins, this shark is a slow swimmer which often feeds on prey that is sleeping or already dead.

These scars were made by bumping against rocks while searching for food and by fighting with other sharks over territory or mates.

GREENLAND SHARK

Somniosus microcephalus

Dogfish shark

Length: 2.4 to 6.4 m (7.9 to 21 ft)
Range: North Atlantic and Arctic Oceans
Habitat: Temperate and Arctic waters to 2,200 m (7,200 ft) deep
Diet: Fish, squid, and seals
Conservation: Vulnerable

Velvet Belly Lanternshark

This small shark is named "velvet belly" for its black underside, which is a different shade from the brown of the rest of the shark's body. Like most dogfish sharks, it has sharp spines on its two dorsal fins, which it uses to defend itself against predators by arching its back.

Lantern of Light

Found in deep, dark water, the 45 species of lanternsharks are named for their ability to make light. The velvet belly lanternshark's belly and sides are dotted with light-making organs known as photophores. When the shark is seen from below, the blue-green lights make it almost invisible against faint sunlight. This form of camouflage is known as counterillumination.

This lanternshark has five pairs of very short gill slits.

The velvet belly's dorsal spines are lit up by its photophores, which is a warning to predators—such as larger sharks and the longnosed skate—that it has weapons and will defend itself.

VELVET BELLY LANTERNSHARK

Etmopterus spinax

Dogfish shark

Length: 40 to 60 cm (16 to 24 in)
Range: Northeastern Atlantic Ocean
Habitat: Tropical and temperate waters to 2,490 m (8,170 ft) deep
Diet: Shrimp, krill, squid, fish, and worms
Conservation: Vulnerable

The long, curved spine on this shark's second dorsal fin is twice as long as the first dorsal fin's spine.

Like other dogfish sharks, the velvet belly lanternshark has no anal fin.

On average, a velvet belly lanternshark has 31 front teeth in its lower jaw and 24 in its upper jaw.

Holding and Cutting

Each small tooth in the velvet belly's upper jaw has up to six cusps (points). These teeth are used for gripping prey. The teeth in the lower jaw are much bigger and squarer. Arranged so they overlap, these bottom teeth form a cutting blade like the edge of a saw. The shark slices flesh using a circular movement of the lower jaw, while the upper jaw holds prey still.

DID YOU KNOW? All velvet belly lanternsharks have the same, particular pattern of lights along their sides, which helps them spot each other at mating time.

Angular Roughshark

Like the four other species of roughsharks, the angular roughshark has extremely rough skin. Its tall, sharp-spined dorsal fins are often caught in fishing nets, leading to this small shark being ranked as endangered.

With its forward-pointing defensive spine, the angular (meaning "sharp cornered") first dorsal fin earns the shark its name.

Shaped for Slowness

Roughsharks have an unusual body shape, flattened and broad at the underside and narrow at the top, making them almost triangular when viewed from the front. For swimming fast, a smoothly shaped, torpedo-like body (narrow at the snout and tail) is ideal for cutting through open water. In contrast, a roughshark's body shape is suited to slow swimming and to hovering over the seafloor as it watches for prey. The shark's flattened underside is ideal for resting on the seafloor for long periods.

A closely related roughshark, the prickly dogfish has tall, sail-like dorsal fins, with the first dorsal fin rising from just behind its eyes.

ANGULAR ROUGHSHARK

Oxynotus centrina

Dogfish shark

Length: 0.5 to 1.5 m (1.6 to 4.9 ft)
Range: Eastern Atlantic Ocean
Habitat: Muddy and algae-covered seafloors in tropical and temperate waters to 660 m (2,170 ft) deep
Diet: Worms, shrimp, fish, and shark eggs
Conservation: Endangered

In this close-up of the sailfin roughshark's skin, we can see that each dermal denticle has four sharp cusps (points): two central, backward-pointing cusps, with a smaller cusp on each side.

Rough Skin

All sharks have rough skin, but the roughsharks have skin with particularly prickly dermal denticles. These help to protect these small sharks from attack. If predators, such as larger sharks, manage to avoid a roughshark's dorsal spines, they will find themselves deeply scraped by the large, knife-like dermal denticles that cover its body.

This shark has such large nostrils, called nares, that scientists think it relies on its sense of smell for detecting prey hiding on the seafloor.

Its pale, fleshy lips are covered in bumps, called papillae, which may contain sensitive cells that help with touching, smelling, and tasting prey.

DID YOU KNOW? The angular roughshark feeds on the contents of shark egg cases, including eggs laid by its own species.

Spiny Dogfish

The spiny dogfish is named for its two sharp spines, one at the front of each dorsal fin. This shark and some of its close relatives in the dogfish shark family are among the only sharks that are venomous.

Venomous Spines

The spiny dogfish makes mild venom, a liquid that causes pain when injected into predators. The venom is produced in glands at the base of the dogfish's spines, so it coats their sharp tips. If the shark is attacked, it curls up, arches its back, and jabs its spines into the predator. This makes most attackers swim away fast. Humans pricked by spiny dogfish report swelling and a burning feeling around the wound.

Dogfish take their name from their habit of hunting in doglike packs, with some packs including over a thousand sharks.

SPINY DOGFISH

Squalus acanthias

Dogfish shark

Length: 0.8 to 1.6 m (2.6 to 5.2 ft)
Range: Atlantic, Indian, Pacific, and Arctic Oceans
Habitat: Temperate and subarctic waters to 700 m (2,300 ft) deep
Diet: Squid, jellyfish, worms, fish, crabs, and shrimp
Conservation: Vulnerable

DID YOU KNOW? Newborn spiny dogfish pups are so aggressive they will attack fish two to three times their size.

This newborn spiny dogfish pup is still attached to its yolk sac.

Longest Pregnancy

This shark has the longest known pregnancy of any shark: 22 to 24 months. The spiny dogfish is ovoviviparous, which means that unborn babies, named embryos, develop inside eggs that remain inside their mother's body. After mating, a shell grows around the fertilized eggs to protect them. After 4 to 6 months, the egg shells are shed but the embryos stay inside their mother, feeding on an attached ball of food, known as a yolk sac. After nearly 2 years, up to 11 pups are born head first, with a sheath covering their spines so the mother is not injured.

This species can be recognized by the small white spots along its back and flanks.

The spiny dogfish usually hunts close to the seafloor.

The shark is countershaded to escape the notice of prey and predators: Its underside is white, while its back and flanks are brown.

Cookiecutter Shark

This shark was named for its habit of biting round chunks of flesh out of large prey, leaving a mark that looks as if it was made by a cookie cutter. These wounds are around 5 cm (2 in) across and 7 cm (2.8 in) deep.

Cookie Bites

Although this shark swallows small prey whole, it takes round bites out of large prey. Its large, triangular bottom teeth form a jagged, saw-like cutting blade. In addition, its lips are large, fleshy, and hardened with cartilage. To take a bite, this shark clamps onto large prey by sucking, forming a tight seal with its lips. Then it bites, using its narrow upper teeth as anchors while it turns its body to make a circular cut. At the same time, this shark vibrates its jaw, creating a movement like an electric carving knife.

With its small dorsal and pectoral fins, this shark is not a fast swimmer, so it hovers while watching for passing prey.

The caudal fin is beaten from side to side when the shark needs a brief burst of speed to attach itself to prey.

Cookiecutter bites can be seen on ocean animals such as humpback whales (pictured), as well as on submarines and underwater cables.

DID YOU KNOW? The cookiecutter loses its lower teeth regularly, then swallows them so their tough calcium can be recycled into new teeth.

COOKIECUTTER SHARK

Isistius brasiliensis

Dogfish shark

Length: 42 to 56 cm (17 to 22 in)
Range: Atlantic, Indian, and Pacific Oceans
Habitat: Around islands in tropical and temperate waters to 3,505 m (11,500 ft) deep
Diet: Bites from whales, dolphins, seals, and fish, as well as whole squid
Conservation: Least concern

Not lit by photophores, this dark collar looks like a small fish when seen from below—and may attract hungry prey within reach of the cookiecutter's jaws.

Making Light

As with other sharks in its kitefin family, the skin of the cookiecutter's belly contains thousands of light-making organs named photophores. These hold tiny lenses and pigments to brighten and tint the light. The photophores make light by mixing together two chemicals made by the shark, creating a chemical reaction (a permanent change) that releases light energy. The ability to make light is known as bioluminescence.

Another member of the kitefin family, the pygmy shark is also bioluminescent. Most kitefins live in the ocean's twilight zone, 200 to 1,000 m (660 to 3,300 ft) below the surface. The water is dimly lit during the day, when the shark's blue light makes it hard to spot. Yet, in total darkness, the shark's light attracts prey.

97

Broadnose Sevengill Shark

This shark is in the Hexanchiformes order of frilled and cow sharks, which have one, spineless dorsal fin and six or seven pairs of gill slits. These are the most primitive sharks: Sharks that looked like modern frilled and cow sharks lived at least 160 million years ago.

Cow Sharks

The broadnose sevengill is one of five living species of cow sharks. With its cow shark relative the sharpnose sevengill, it shares the record for the shark with most gill slits. Only sharks in the Hexanchiformes order and the sixgill sawsharks have more than five pairs of gill slits. The cow sharks are named for their usually round, blunt snouts, which make them look a little like cows. They have wide, comb-shaped teeth in their lower jaw, for tearing prey, and sharp, jagged teeth in their upper jaw, for holding wriggling prey.

Like other cow sharks, the broadnose sevengill has only one, small dorsal fin, as well as a caudal fin with a much larger upper than lower lobe.

BROADNOSE SEVENGILL SHARK

Notorynchus cepedianus

Frilled and cow shark

Length: 1.5 to 3 m (4.9 to 9.8 ft)
Range: Atlantic, Indian, and Pacific Oceans
Habitat: Coastal tropical and temperate waters to 1,870 ft (570 m) deep
Diet: Fish, seals, crabs, snails, and octopus
Conservation: Vulnerable

This broadnose sevengill is swimming through a kelp forest near the coast of South Africa.

As its name suggests, this cow shark has a very unusual number of pairs of gill slits: seven.

The broadnose sevengill is countershaded and has black and white speckles across its whole body to help with camouflage.

Frilled Sharks

The frilled shark family contains just two living species: the frilled shark and the southern African frilled shark. These rare sharks take their name from the puckered appearance of their six pairs of gill slits. The frilled sharks have long, snake-like bodies that bend and wiggle as they swim. Their stomachs and mouths can expand to swallow prey more than half the size of the shark itself. Neither shark grows longer than 2 m (6.6 ft) long.

A frilled shark's jaws contain 300 three-pointed teeth. The rows of teeth are widely spaced, with up to 28 rows in the upper jaw and up to 29 in the lower jaw.

DID YOU KNOW? The broadnose sevengill shark often scavenges, eating dead animals that are floating in the water or lying on the seafloor.

Horn Shark

This shark is a member of the bullhead shark order. These small, nocturnal sharks are named for their bull-like appearance: a large head in comparison with their body, along with a ridge above each eye shaped rather like a bull's horn.

The horn shark has spines more than 5 cm (2 in) long.

Sharp Spines

The bullhead sharks have a long spine at the front of each of their two tall dorsal fins. The spines are made of dentine and covered by enameloid, which are extremely strong, hard materials also found in human teeth. By curling and twisting their body, the bullhead sharks use their spines to defend themselves against predators. In addition, predators such as angelsharks have been seen spitting out horn sharks after finding their spines too sharp to swallow.

The horn shark's supraorbital ridge is covered by extra-large, thick dermal denticles.

Brow Ridges

Like most bottom-dwellers, bullhead sharks have eyes positioned high on their head to give a better view over algae and rocks. Like many small animals, their eyes are also on their sides of their head so they can watch all around for predators. The thick, bony ridge above each eye, known as a supraorbital (meaning "above eye") ridge, shields the eyes from the glare of sunlight. It also makes the bright eyes harder to spot by predators swimming overhead.

DID YOU KNOW? Compared with its body size, the horn shark has the strongest bite of any shark—which it uses for crushing shells.

HORN SHARK

Heterodontus francisci

Bullhead shark

Length: 0.8 to 1.2 m (2.6 to 3.9 ft)
Range: Coasts of Mexico and the United States in the Pacific Ocean
Habitat: Rocky reefs and algae beds in tropical waters to 200 m (660 ft) deep
Diet: Oysters, sea urchins, shrimp, crabs, and small fish
Conservation: Unknown

During the day, this shark rests on thick mats of algae, where its golden-brown, spotted body is well camouflaged.

Bullhead sharks have a wide snout with large, trumpet-like nostrils, which help these bottom-dwellers to smell prey.

The horn shark relies less on electroreception to find prey, as it has only 148 ampullae of Lorenzini, compared with more than 2,000 in some sharks.

Japanese Bullhead Shark

The Japanese bullhead is a slow-moving, sluggish shark. It feeds on bottom-living, hard-shelled prey, which it grinds up with its strong back teeth before swallowing—but it usually brings up and spits out big bits of shell later.

Spiral Egg Cases

Like other bullhead sharks, the Japanese bullhead lays eggs. Bullhead shark egg cases are differently shaped from those of other sharks. Their egg cases are cone-shaped, with a large ridge twisting around the outside. Like the twisting groove on a screw, this shape anchors the eggs in crevices among rocks and coral, so they cannot be removed by predators.

While it lies on the bottom, the Japanese bullhead shark sucks in water through its spiracle so its gills can continue to take oxygen.

It takes several hours for a female Japanese bullhead shark to lay each egg, due to the awkward, ridged shape of its case.

JAPANESE BULLHEAD SHARK

Heterodontus japonicus

Bullhead shark

Length: 0.7 to 1.2 m (2.3 to 3.9 ft)
Range: Coasts of Japan, Korea, and China in the Pacific Ocean
Habitat: Coral reefs, rocky seafloors, and kelp forests in temperate waters to 37 m (121 ft) deep
Diet: Sea urchins, snails, shrimp, crabs, and small fish
Conservation: Least concern

The Japanese bullhead rests during the day, then hunts at night, often "walking" across the seafloor using its wide pectoral and pelvic fins.

Little Mouth

The bullhead sharks have little mouths that are positioned at the front of their snouts. Such mouths are suited to picking up or sucking up small, slow-moving prey. These sharks have small, cone-shaped front teeth that are used for grasping. Their back teeth are round, broad, and flat, making them ideal for crushing shells.

Like other bullhead sharks, the crested bullhead shark has a small mouth, which is joined to its nostrils by deep grooves.

This shark is camouflaged by dark bands that break up its outline, making it harder for predators to spot.

DID YOU KNOW? Female Japanese bullheads lay their eggs in the same patch as other females in their school, making them one of the few sharks to share a nest.

Longnose Sawshark

Like other members of the sawshark order, the longnose sawshark has a saw-like snout known as a rostrum, which it uses to catch prey. Its rostrum is the longest among all the sawsharks, reaching a length of 40 cm (16 in).

Digging Rostrum

A longnose sawshark's rostrum is edged with sharp teeth, which alternate between long and short. Like the teeth inside the shark's mouth, these teeth are replaced when they fall out. The teeth help to stir up the sand as the sawshark uses its rostrum to dig in the seafloor for small, hiding prey. The sawshark also uses its rostrum to swipe at swimming fish by waving it quickly from side to side— stunning and slashing prey with its weight and teeth.

The longnose sawshark can live for up to 15 years.

A longnose sawshark's rostrum is dotted with tiny ampullae of Lorenzini (see page 16), which detect the electric fields created by moving prey.

DID YOU KNOW? Female longnose sawsharks give birth to live pups, which have the teeth along their rostrum folded inward so they do not injure their mother.

Having a Rest

Schools of longnose sawsharks spend the daytime resting on the seafloor, where they are well camouflaged by their sandy, blotchy dermal denticles. When predators pass, a sawshark's flattened body lets it lie low. Sawshark predators include larger sharks, such as great whites, as well as human beings.

Longnose sawsharks can often be seen raised on their pectoral fins on the seafloor, giving them a wide view of the surrounding area.

At the middle of the rostrum is a pair of sensitive barbels, which the sawshark uses to feel, taste, and smell prey hiding in sand and gravel.

Unlike sawfish, which have gill slits on the underside of their head, sawsharks have gill slits on the sides of their head.

LONGNOSE SAWSHARK

Pristiophorus cirratus

Sawshark

Length: 1 to 1.3 m (3.3 to 4.3 ft)
Range: Coast of southern Australia in the Indian and Pacific Oceans
Habitat: Sandy or gravel seafloors in temperate waters to 310 m (1,017 ft) deep
Diet: Small fish, shrimp, crabs, and squid
Conservation: Least concern

Japanese Angelshark

The angelsharks take their name from their wide pectoral fins, which are said to look like angels' wings. Like its relatives, the Japanese angelshark is an ambush predator that lies in wait for prey, although it may swim in search of food at night.

The wide pectoral and pelvic fins are held horizontally as the shark swims, powered largely by its long, waving tail.

Hiding …

During the day, Japanese angelsharks bury themselves in the seafloor. They do this by slapping the ground with their body and pectoral and pelvic fins, sending up showers of sand and pebbles until they are hidden. Their speckled skin and flattened body shape also help to keep them camouflaged.

Only the Japanese angelshark's eyes are left uncovered, so it can watch for prey.

JAPANESE ANGELSHARK

Squatina japonica

Angelshark

Length: 1.5 to 2 m (4.9 to 6.6 ft)
Range: Coasts of Japan, Korea, and China in the Pacific Ocean
Habitat: Sandy seafloors in temperate waters to 300 m (980 ft) deep
Diet: Fish, shrimp, octopus, and squid
Conservation: Critically endangered

DID YOU KNOW? This angelshark is fished for its skin, known as shagreen, which is used to cover items such as photo frames and decorative boxes.

Unusually for a shark, the lower lobe of the caudal fin is slightly longer than the upper lobe.

... And Attacking

When a Japanese angelshark senses approaching prey, it lunges upward from its hiding place and shoots out its jaws, which can swing both upward and outward. Like those of all sharks, its jaws are not fixed to its skull. The shark sucks prey into its mouth, pinning and ripping with its sharp, cone-shaped teeth.

This Japanese angelshark has flexed its neck and thrust out its jaws to catch a silver-stripe round herring.

Cartilaginous Fish

Unlike other fish, sharks and their close relatives have skeletons made of light, bendy cartilage rather than bone. Known as cartilaginous fish, they make up a class of fish known as Chondrichthyes.

The bowmouth guitarfish is in the Rhinopristiformes order of rays, in the Elasmobranchii subclass of the Chondrichthyes class of fish.

First Fish

Tiny, simple living things appeared in Earth's oceans around 3.5 billion years ago. Through slow changes, known as evolution, the first fishlike animals were swimming by 530 million years ago. Early fish had cartilage-like skeletons and no jaws, so they could not bite. Today's fish are in three groups known as classes: Agnatha, containing 120 species that still have a cartilaginous skeleton and no jaws; Chondrichthyes, containing around 1,050 species that evolved jaws but have a cartilaginous skeleton; and Osteichthyes, with 33,000 species of jawed fish that evolved bony skeletons.

Although it did not have a well-defined head, *Pikaia* was a fishlike animal that lived between 513 and 505 million years ago.

BOWMOUTH GUITARFISH

Rhina ancylostoma

Rhinopristiform ray

Length: 1.5 to 2.7 m (4.9 to 8.9 ft)
Range: Indian and Pacific Oceans
Habitat: Sandy and muddy seafloors in tropical waters to 90 m (300 ft) deep
Diet: Fish, crabs, shrimp, and clams
Conservation: Critically endangered

DID YOU KNOW? The bowmouth guitarfish is fished for its meat, fins, and thornlike dermal denticles, which are used to make bracelets.

Class of Chondrichthyes

Unlike bony-skeletoned fish, Chondrichthyes do not have a gas-filled organ known as a swim bladder to help them float. All Chondrichthyes can sense the electric fields given off by prey using organs known as ampullae of Lorenzini. The Chondrichthyes are divided into two subclasses: Elasmobranchii, containing sharks and rays; and Holocephali, containing chimaeras. Like sharks, most rays have replaceable teeth, toothlike scales, and visible gill slits. Unlike sharks, most rays have a flattened body with gill slits on the underside. Chimaeras do not have replaceable teeth, toothlike scales, or visible gill slits.

Extinct Sharks

The earliest sharks evolved around 420 million years ago, long before the first trees, flowers, dinosaurs, or monkeys. Like modern sharks, ancient sharks had cartilaginous skeletons, toothlike scales, and teeth that were replaced when they fell out.

Up to 20.3 m (67 ft) long, *Megalodon* (meaning "big tooth") was the largest shark ever known to exist. It lived between 23 and 3.6 million years ago.

Shark Fossils

Fossils tell us how ancient sharks looked. By studying features such as their tooth and fin shapes, we can make guesses about what and how they ate. Shark fossils formed when dead sharks sank to the water bottom and were buried quickly in sand or mud. The sharks' soft body parts, such as flesh and skin, usually rotted away. Over thousands of years, mineral-rich water seeped into the hard parts of the shark's body, slowly replacing the tooth or cartilage with minerals.

This rare fossil has preserved an image of the shark's whole body, as minerals in its skin and scales left behind a print on the rock.

Megalodon took in water through its mouth and soaked up oxygen using gills, before the water flowed out of five gill slits.

MEGALODON

Otodus megalodon

Mackerel shark

Length: 14 to 20.3 m (46 to 67 ft)
Range: Atlantic, Indian, and Pacific Oceans
Habitat: Tropical and temperate waters possibly to 1,000 m (3,280 ft) deep
Diet: Whales, seals, and sea turtles
Conservation: Extinct

This shark beat its crescent-shaped tail to power through the oceans at perhaps 18 km/h (11 mph).

Freshwater Sharks

Most modern sharks are found in saltwater, but dozens of extinct sharks lived only or mostly in freshwater. Like their ocean-living relatives, many freshwater sharks were apex predators, so large and sharp-toothed they were rarely attacked unless they were young or sick.

Living around 260 million years ago, *Orthacanthus* was an apex predator in freshwater swamps of Europe and North America. This shark grew up to 3 m (9.8 ft) long and was armed with a spike that stopped predators from biting its neck and head.

DID YOU KNOW? *Megalodon* became extinct because of cooling oceans and a drop in the number of small whales that were its main food.

Guitarfish

Guitarfish are named for their flattened, guitar-shaped body. They are in the family of rays known as Rhinobatidae (meaning "nose ray"), due to having a longer snout than most rays. Around 36 guitarfish species live in tropical to warm temperate oceans close to coasts.

A Ray's Underside

Like most rays, guitarfish have their mouth on their underside, which is useful for sucking up small animals that live in or on the seafloor. Since guitarfish spend much of their time lying on the seafloor, they do not breathe by taking in water through their mouth but by sucking it through their spiracles, which are holes behind their eyes on the upper side of their body. The used water passes out of gill slits. Unlike sharks, which have their gill slits on the sides of their head, rays have gill slits under their pectoral fins.

Guitarfish and other rays have wide pectoral fins that are fused to their body.

Nostrils

Mouth

Gill slits

Pectoral fin

Cloaca

Pelvic fin

Pee and poop pass out of a guitarfish's cloaca. Like other rays, a guitarfish has no anal fin.

DID YOU KNOW? Guitarfish have been swimming in the oceans for at least the past 94 million years.

In low light, a banded guitarfish's pupils are large and round, but in bright light a tough, shiny tissue containing cartilage prevents too much light entering the eye.

Unusual Eyes

Guitarfish eyes have pupils (holes through which light passes into the eye) that narrow in bright light until they form a shape like a scribbled W. This shape is useful in shallow water, where it is often sunny above and dim below, as it evens out glare and shadow. Since guitarfish cannot close their eyelids, they pull their eyeballs 4 cm (1.6 in) back into their head to protect them when burrowing in sand or attacking prey.

Unlike most rays, guitarfish swim by moving their caudal (tail) fin from side to side, in the same manner as many sharks.

The Gorgona guitarfish's speckled, blotchy dermal denticles keep it camouflaged as it waits for bottom-living prey.

GORGONA GUITARFISH

Pseudobatos prahli

Rhinopristiform ray

Length: 70 to 90 cm (28 to 35 in)
Range: Coasts of Central and South America in the eastern Pacific Ocean
Habitat: Sandy and rocky seafloors in tropical waters to 70 m (230 ft) deep
Diet: Crabs, shrimp, worms, and clams
Conservation: Vulnerable

Sawfish

These rays have a saw-like snout, known as a rostrum. The rostrum is dotted with thousands of ampullae of Lorenzini, which are organs that sense the electric fields made by moving prey. When prey is detected, sawfish use their sharp-edged rostrum for swiping and pinning.

Sawfish vs Sawsharks

Sawfish are often confused with sawsharks, due to their similar-looking rostrums. However, sawfish are more closely related to other rays than to sawsharks. The similarity between sawfish and sawsharks is an example of convergent (meaning "coming closer together") evolution, which is when two different groups of animals evolve to have the same features because they are useful for the same purpose: in this case, finding and catching prey using their snout.

Up to 140 cm (55 in) long, the rostrum is made of cartilage covered in skin.

Along each side of its rostrum, the smalltooth sawfish has up to 32 "teeth," which are actually enlarged dermal denticles that are not replaced if they fall out.

Unlike a sawshark, a sawfish (pictured) has gill slits on its underside. The teeth along a sawfish's rostrum are all the same length, while a sawshark's alternate between long and short. Sawfish do not have sensory barbels on their rostrum, but sawsharks do.

DID YOU KNOW? Sawfish are among the world's most endangered fish, due to overfishing and damage to the shallow coastal habitats where females give birth.

SMALLTOOTH SAWFISH

Pristis pectinata

Rhinopristiform ray

Length: 5 to 5.5 m (16.4 to 18 ft)
Range: Atlantic Ocean
Habitat: Coastal seafloors in tropical and subtropical waters to 122 m (400 ft) deep
Diet: Fish, shrimp, and crabs
Conservation: Critically endangered

The smalltooth sawfish often rests on the seafloor, while the ampullae of Lorenzini along the top of its rostrum detect prey swimming overhead.

Sawfish Magic

For thousands of years, people living in coastal regions have told stories, created art, and performed dances about sawfish. Due to their strange rostrum, sawfish have been seen as magical, dangerous, and linked with the world of spirits and gods. In Africa's Gambia, sawfish rostrums were displayed in homes as symbols of fishermen's bravery. In Southeast Asia, they were hung over doorways to keep out ghosts. In Nigeria and the Bissagos Islands of Guinea-Bissau, dancers wore sawfish masks during ceremonies and celebrations.

This African sawfish mask was made from wood and shell in the early 20th century.

River Stingrays

Unlike most rays, the river stingrays usually live in freshwater. They are found in South American rivers, where they often lie on the bottom, partly buried in sand or mud. When prey nears, these fish raise their head by pressing down with their pectoral fins, then suck hard with their mouth.

This stingray's stinger is covered in a sheath of skin and hooked dermal denticles that widen any wound made by the sting.

Stinging Spine

A stingray has one or two sharp spines on its tail. The spines are covered in venom, a liquid that causes pain, swelling, and infection if it is injected into predators by a prick from the spine. Stingrays use their spines only to defend themselves, but sometimes human swimmers and waders are stung when they fail to spot stingrays buried on the river floor.

A stingray's stinger is usually covered by skin, which rips open when the stinger is used (pictured). The fish stings by waving its tail so the spine pierces its own skin covering and pricks the predator's skin.

POLKA DOT STINGRAY

Potamotrygon leopoldi

Myliobatiform ray

Length: 30 to 75 cm (12 to 30 in)
Range: Xingu and Fresco Rivers in Brazil, South America
Habitat: Sandy floors in tropical river water
Diet: Snails and crabs
Conservation: Not known

Waving Along

Unlike sharks, which usually swim by beating their caudal fin, stingrays swim by waving their wide, curving pectoral fins. Waves of movement travel along the pectoral fins from front to back. This swimming style does not create fast movement, but it also does not use a lot of energy.

Turns are made by waving one pectoral fin more than the other, but stingrays' wide, flattened bodies are not suited to sudden changes of direction.

The polka dot stingray's disk-shaped body is up to 40 cm (16 in) wide.

When lying on the river floor, a stingray takes in water through its spiracles rather than its mouth.

DID YOU KNOW? Stingrays shed and replace their venomous spine every 6 to 12 months, with the new spine often growing while the old one is still in place.

Mobula Rays

These rays are often called "flying rays" due to their habit of leaping out of the water, known as breaching. The mobula family includes the devil rays and manta rays, which are famed both for their great size and their great intelligence.

Clever Fish

With a brain weighing up to 200 g (7 oz), the giant oceanic manta ray has the heaviest brain compared to its body weight of any fish. These rays show their intelligence by playing with and forming friendships with others in their school. When manta rays meet an unknown manta, the white patches on their shoulders brighten. Yet when shown their reflection in a mirror, the white patches stay the same, as manta rays seem to recognize the reflection as themselves. This "mirror test" is not passed by most animals or even by very young humans.

Giant oceanic manta rays often go together to areas known as "cleaning stations," where fish, such as remoras, feed on their irritating parasites.

MUNK'S DEVIL RAY

Mobula munkiana

Myliobatiform ray

Length: 1 to 2.2 m (3.3 to 7.2 ft)
Range: Eastern Pacific Ocean
Habitat: Tropical waters to 15 m (49 ft) deep
Diet: Zooplankton, shrimp, and small fish
Conservation: Vulnerable

DID YOU KNOW? Up to 7 m (23 ft) across, the giant oceanic manta ray is one of the largest fish, with only a few species of sharks growing bigger.

Like other mobula rays, the Munk's devil ray jumps to show off to a mate, to communicate with its school, or to knock parasites off its body as it slaps back down.

Fine Fins

Mobula rays swim by moving their triangular pectoral fins up and down, like a bird flapping its wings. The pectoral fins have horn-shaped extensions, known as cephalic fins, on either side of the ray's mouth. When mobula rays are feeding, they stretch their cephalic fins forward to funnel water into their open mouth and through their gills. Mobula rays are filter feeders: They filter tiny animals, known as zooplankton, out of the water using sieve-like pads in their mouth. Water flows out through the gills, while food is caught on the pads.

Munk's devil rays have a long, stingless tail, which is not used for swimming or steering.

As a manta ray feeds, it flies through the water by flapping its pectoral fins, sending water into its open mouth.

Electric Rays

The electric rays make electricity, which they use to stun prey and defend themselves. Like other rays, electric rays have a flattened body and large pectoral fins. Yet, unlike other rays and sharks, these fish have soft skin with no covering of dermal denticles.

Making Electricity

An electric ray has two large electricity-making organs, on either side of its head. Each organ contains thousands of cells named electrocytes, which make electricity by stimulating electrically charged atoms. The electric charge travels into the surrounding water. The power of an electric ray's organs ranges from 8 to 220 volts. Household electricity has a force of around 230 volts in most of the world. The most powerful organs belong to the Atlantic torpedo, which emits enough electricity to stun large predators.

The panther torpedo ray's rounded pectoral fins, which are fused with its head and body, form an almost circular disk.

The outlines of the leopard torpedo's electricity-making organs can be seen on the underside of its body.

Most rays swim by waving their pectoral fins, but the slow-moving electric rays swim by waving their caudal fin.

PANTHER TORPEDO RAY

Torpedo panthera

Torpediniform ray

Length: 28 to 98 cm (11 to 39 in)
Range: Western Indian Ocean
Habitat: Coral reefs and muddy or sandy seafloors in tropical waters to 100 m (328 ft) deep
Diet: Small fish, shrimp, and crabs
Conservation: Not known

Pouncing on Prey

Electric rays spend much of their time resting on the seafloor, usually partly buried in sand. When small fish or other little animals pass by, electric rays pounce, wrapping their body around them while delivering a strong electric shock. The stunned prey is moved into the ray's mouth using rippling movements of its pectoral fins.

The marbled electric ray buries itself on the seafloor, leaving only its eyes and spiracles exposed.

The torpedo rays take their name from the Latin word *torpidus* ("paralysed"), due to making small pulses of electricity to warn away predators or large, stunning shocks.

DID YOU KNOW? Ancient Greek doctors used electric rays to deliver numbing shocks to patients just before operating on them.

Skates

Skates are a family of rays with a kite-shaped body and a stiff snout. Their long, slender tail contains an electricity-making organ. Unlike the electric rays, skates can make only a weak electric charge, which may be used for attracting the attention of a mate.

Safe on the Seafloor

Skates are bottom-dwellers, spending most of their time lying on the seafloor, partly buried in sand or gravel, or gliding close to the bottom as they search for prey. Skates are well camouflaged from both prey and predators by having flattened bodies covered in sandy, speckled dermal denticles. In addition, many skates have eyespots (markings shaped like eyes) on the upper side of their pectoral fins, which frighten away predators.

Tall, thornlike dermal denticles surrounding the head give protection from predators.

The large eyespots of the Velez skate make predators think the skate is much larger than it is.

DID YOU KNOW? Little skates have been seen walking over the seafloor using first their left pelvic fin and then their right.

Old, empty skate egg cases are often found washed up on beaches.

Horned Egg Cases

Unlike their ray relatives, which give birth to live pups, skates lay eggs. These are protected by tough, leathery egg cases. Most skate species lay small cases, around 8 cm (3 in) long, containing one egg. Yet some skates lay larger cases holding up to seven eggs. Skate egg cases are more rectangular than those of egg-laying sharks. They have a curving horn at each corner, which catches on seaweed or rocks to stop them drifting into deep waters. The egg cases are waterproof at first, but soon after the growing babies have developed gills, holes open in the tips of the horns, letting seawater flow inside.

A little skate's 38 to 66 rows of small, round teeth are suited to crushing shelled prey.

The little skate's mouth is surrounded by ampullae of Lorenzini, which help it home in on small creatures hiding in the sand and gravel.

LITTLE SKATE

Leucoraja erinacea

Rajiform ray

Length: 41 to 54 cm (16 to 21 in)
Range: Northwestern Atlantic Ocean
Habitat: Sandy or gravel seafloors in temperate waters to 90 m (300 ft) deep
Diet: Crabs, shrimp, and worms
Conservation: Least concern

Chimaeras

These strange fish are usually found in deep, dark ocean water. In Greek myths, chimaeras were monsters with body parts of different animals, such as a lion's head and a serpent's tail. Real-life chimaeras have a large head, with a ducklike snout, and a long, slender tail.

A female rabbit fish lives for up to 26 years and is able to lay eggs once she is 11 years old.

A Different Path

Chimaeras share the cartilaginous skeleton of sharks and rays, but around 400 million years ago, the ancestors of chimaeras started to evolve differently from their relatives. Unlike sharks and most rays, chimaeras have naked, rubbery skin without a covering of dermal denticles. They also do not have replaceable teeth, instead having three pairs of permanent tooth plates suited to grinding. Rather than five to seven pairs of visible gill slits, they have one pair of gill slits protected by covers, like the bony fish.

The spotted ratfish, like other chimaeras, has large eyes for seeing in dim water close to the ocean floor.

DID YOU KNOW? For attracting or holding females, male chimaeras have small spiky clubs that can be folded out from their forehead.

RABBIT FISH

Chimaera monstrosa

Holocephali

Length: 0.4 to 1.5 m (1.3 to 4.9 ft)
Range: Northeastern Atlantic Ocean
Habitat: Close to the seafloor in temperate waters
to 1,400 m (4,590 ft) deep
Diet: Crabs, worms, octopus, and sea urchins
Conservation: Vulnerable

The venomous spine is raised to prick predators and lowered while swimming.

Chimaeras swim by flapping their winglike pectoral fins as they wiggle their long body.

Significant Spines

To protect them from predators, chimaeras have a sharp spine at the front of their first dorsal fin. It is covered in mild venom that causes pain when injected. Many fossils of ancient chimaera spines have been found, suggesting there were more chimaeras in the past than today, some of them living in shallow water. Today, there are only around 50 chimaera species.

The smallspine spookfish has a venomous spine up to 10 cm (4 in) long. Its snout is dotted with ampullae of Lorenzini that help it find prey

Glossary

AGGREGATION
A gathering of sharks or other living things, often at a particular time of year or place.

ALGAE
Simple plantlike living things that usually live in and around water, such as seaweeds.

AMPULLAE OF LORENZINI
Organs—found in sharks, rays, and chimaeras—that can detect the electric fields made by animals' muscles as they move.

ANAL FIN
A fin on a fish's underside, toward the tail.

ATOM
The smallest portion of any material that can exist on its own.

BARBEL
A whisker-like body part on the snout which helps fish to taste and smell prey.

CAMOUFLAGE
The way the shade, pattern, and shape of an animal make it less visible in its habitat.

CARTILAGE
A body material that is strong, bendy, and lightweight.

CAUDAL FIN
The tail fin.

CELL
The smallest working part of a living thing.

CEPHALOFOIL
The outward extensions of the head of a shark in the hammerhead family.

CHIMAERA
A fish with a skeleton made of cartilage, bare skin, and a single, covered gill opening.

CLASS
A scientific group that includes animals with the same body plan, such as bony-skeletoned or cartilaginous fish.

CORAL REEF
An underwater structure made by groups of tiny animals named coral polyps, which build hard skeletons around their soft bodies.

COUNTERSHADING
A form of camouflage in which an animal is darker on its upperside and paler on its underside, making it harder to spot when viewed from above or below in sunlit water.

CRITICALLY ENDANGERED
Describes a species that is at extremely high risk of becoming extinct soon.

DERMAL DENTICLE
A pointed scale found on the skin of sharks and most rays, with a similar structure and materials to teeth.

DORSAL FIN
A fin on the upper side of a fish, with sharks having one or two.

ELECTRIC FIELD
An area around an electric charge in which its force can be felt.

ENDANGERED
Describes a species that is likely to become extinct in the near future.

ESTUARY
The mouth of a large river, where it meets the ocean.

EVOLVE
To change gradually over time.

FAMILY
A scientific group that includes genera similar to each other.

FILTER FEEDING
Straining food from the water using comb- or net-like mouthparts.

FIN
A body part that juts from the body of fish, helping them swim.

FISH
A water-living animal that takes oxygen from the water using gills and usually has fins.

FRESHWATER
Unsalted water, such as rivers, lakes, and ponds.

GENUS (PLURAL GENERA)
A scientific group that includes species very similar to each other.

GILL
An organ in fish that takes oxygen from water.

GILL SLIT
An uncovered opening to a gill that can be seen in sharks and rays.

HABITAT
The natural home of an animal, plant, or other living thing.

LEAST CONCERN
Describes a species that is not currently at risk of extinction.

LOBE
A division of a body part, such as the upper and lower portions of a caudal fin.

MATE
A male or female partner for making babies.

MIGRATION
A seasonal or daily movement of animals from one region to another.

MINERAL
A solid that forms in the ground or in water.

NEAR THREATENED
Describes a species that is likely to become endangered in the near future.

NICTITATING MEMBRANE
A third, see-through eyelid that protects a groundshark's eyeball.

ORDER
A scientific group that includes families similar to each other.

ORGAN
A body part that does a particular job, such as the heart or brain.

OVERFISHING
Catching so many of a particular fish that the species drops dramatically in number.

OXYGEN
A gas found in air and water which is needed by animals' cells to make energy to do their work.

PARASITE
A living thing that lives in or on another living thing.

PECTORAL FIN
One of a pair of fins on either side of a fish, behind its head.

PELVIC FIN
One of a pair of fins on a fish's underside, toward its tail.

PIGMENT
A substance that gives colour.

POLAR
In the cold regions around the North and South Pole, in the Arctic and Southern Oceans.

PREDATOR
An animal that hunts other animals.

PREY
An animal that is killed by another animal for food.

PUPIL
The opening in an eye that lets in light. Light bounces off objects and into the eye, where it stimulates cells that message the brain.

RAY
A fish with a skeleton made of cartilage, a flattened body, five or six gill slits on its underside, and usually skin covered by dermal denticles.

SCALE
A small, hard plate that protects the skin of most fish.

SCHOOL
A group of sharks.

SCLERA
The outer layer of the eye.

SEASONAL
Happening at a particular time of year.

SHARK
A fish with a skeleton made of cartilage, five to seven gill slits on the sides of its head, and skin covered by dermal denticles.

SNOUT
The part of an animal's head containing the nose and jaws.

SPECIES
A group of living things that look similar and can mate together.

SPIRACLE
Found in some sharks and rays, a hole behind each eye that lets water pass into the gills.

SUBARCTIC
In the cold area just to the south of the Arctic.

SUBTROPICAL
In the areas to the south or north of the tropics, where the ocean is fairly warm all year.

TEMPERATE
In the areas between the subtropics and polar regions, where the ocean ranges from cold to warm.

THREATENED
At risk of extinction in the future.

TIDE
The rising and falling of the ocean at the shore, caused by the pull of the Moon's gravity on the water.

TROPICAL
In the area around the equator, where the water is warm all year.

VENOMOUS
Able to give a poisoned bite or sting.

VULNERABLE
Describes a species that is at risk of extinction in the medium term.

ZOOPLANKTON
Tiny animals and eggs that drift through the water.

Index